O. W. WILSON AND THE SEARCH FOR A POLICE PROFESSION

Kennikat Press
National University Publications
Interdisciplinary Urban Series

General Editor
Raymond A. Mohl
Florida Atlantic University

William J. Bopp

O. W. Wilson and the
Search for a
Police Profession

WITHDRAWN

National University Publications
KENNIKAT PRESS   //   1977
Port Washington, N. Y.   //   London

Manufactured in the United States of America

Published by
Kennikat Press Corp.
Port Washington, N. Y./London

Library of Congress Cataloging in Publication Data

Bopp, William J
     "O. W.": O. W. Wilson and the search for a Police
Profession.

     (National university publications) (Interdisciplinary
urban series)
     Bibliography: p.
     Includes index.
     1. Wilson, Orlando Winfield, 1900–1972. 2. Police—
United States—Biography. 3. Police administration—
United States—History. I. Title.
HV7911.W54B66   363.2'092'4 [B]   77-329
ISBN 0-8046-9179-7
ISBN 0-8046-9201-7 (paper)

CONTENTS

PREFACE

In America, the balance between police power and citizen rights is constantly being redefined. Crime, violence, and civil disorder have led to public clamor for law and order and to court decisions offsetting the injudicious actions of overzealous police officers. Great, and often conflicting, demands are made on the police. They are expected to protect and serve communities which often look down upon them. They are ordered to enforce laws which have for centuries been unenforceable. They have been thrust into the midst of complex social problems and told to ameliorate them with coercive methods of control. They have been brutalized by citizens, abused by the press, and exploited by politicians. They have often become their own worst enemies by conspiring with criminals, by using excessive force on citizens, and by taking a cavalier attitude toward civil liberties. Yet, it is indisputable that today more than ever we need competent, democratic police forces committed to a service ideal, responsive to human problems.

American law enforcement is in a period of appraisal. The movement to professionalize the police is in large measure a search for identity. Much of the literature in journals and in texts is devoted to a definition of the role of the police in a democratic society. Central to this definition are certain fundamental questions which have not been satisfactorily answered: To whom are the police directly responsible? What constitutes police work? How should officers be evaluated? Which level of government should control them? To what extent should individual liberty be surrendered in return for police protection? Scholars are in the process of answering these and other questions, but it is clear that police administrators, because of the unique place they occupy, will be the pivotal figures in eventually defining the role of the police.

It has become commonplace for public officials to grant chiefs of police almost complete independence to operate their departments. The historical link between police corruption and partisan politics has been so dramatic that police autonomy has become something of a civic virtue. As a consequence, chiefs often pursue their daily responsibilities uninhibited by oversight from public officials frightened of being accused of interfering with the police. This abdication of authority has placed in the hands of police administrators unprecedented power to make and shape sensitive public policy affecting the safety, security, morals, and liberties of citizens. Notwithstanding the grave implications this has for the country, it has also propelled chiefs of police into positions of incredible importance in society.

In spite of the power that has been delegated to police administrators, very little is known about the people who actually wield it. With the exception of writings about J. Edgar Hoover, there has been a dearth of material on police leadership. Even in Hoover's case, much of the information on him has been supplied by writers who appear to be more preoccupied with either canonizing a saint or burning a witch than uncovering facts. Reliable biographical information on police administrators is all but nonexistent. It is a void which should be filled, and one toward which this volume was directed.

Orlando Winfield Wilson was America's most influential police scholar and administrator. For precisely that reason, Wilson was selected for study. In many respects, his professional life is a history of law enforcement in microcosm, for it deals with the political realities of police administration, the recurring problem of corruption, the often abrasive impact of reform, the nature of police-community relations, the development of a police literature and opportunities for higher education, and with the historical and contemporary movements to professionalize the police.

I never met Orlando Wilson personally, though as an undergraduate student and young policeman studying for promotion, his reputation as superintendent of police in Chicago and his writings became well known to me. Later, as a professor who almost instinctively adopted *Police Administration,* I became interested in Wilson the man. When he died in 1973, I approached his widow, Ruth Elinor Wilson, to ask permission to be Wilson's biographer. She agreed.

Wilson was a difficult subject to write about. He was a private person and did not usually share his feelings with other people, even family members. A teenage nickname of "Windy" was facetiously bestowed by friends because of his avoidance of conversation. He outgrew a childhood shyness, but never became an open, gregarious man. Nevertheless, there is sufficient data available for a comprehensive and effective biography of Wilson. Whether or not this volume is a comprehensive, effective work is a judgment best left to others. In any event, there was no shortage of research material.

It is quite appropriate that I acknowledge some of the many people who have helped in this project. Contrariwise, although it may not be good form to criticize those who hindered my efforts, I intend to do so anyway, in the belief that candor should outweigh courtesy, at least in this case, and in hopes that public criticism may make some future scholar's job a little easier. To Mrs. Ruth Elinor Wilson, who granted me permission to undertake this project, who completely cooperated in it, and who suffered through many hours of long interviews, despite being ill at the time, I am profoundly grateful. I hope that I have done her "Win" justice and have not been too harsh in my occasional criticism of him. My thanks to the rest of the Wilson family for their cooperation, especially Patricia Anne.

I appreciate the Wichita Police Department's assistance in locating research material. Captain Dick Cole was particularly helpful in the search for facts. As for the Chicago Police Department, I hope that other researchers have better luck at penetrating the bureaucratic veil which it uses as a protection against outsiders.

Franklin Kreml was of great value in studying Wilson's Chicago years. But rather than single out one source, I would like to express my sincere gratitude for the hours all interviewees set aside for me. The personal interviews represent the core of this research effort. It is a tribute to their affection and admiration for O. W. Wilson that they were so eager to contribute to his biography. Their names are listed in the bibliography of this work. Each contributed something unique.

My thanks to historian John O'Sullivan, and Professors Joe Cook, Bob Kite, Dan Weppner, and Steve Hartman for taking the time to painstakingly read and correct the myriad mistakes in the early drafts. Their criticism was always constructive and welcome. Barbara MacDougall's patience in doing the secretarial and clerical work is deeply appreciated. Great cooperation was received from the staffs of the Florida Atlantic University Library, the Chicago Public Library, and the Witchita Public Library.

I would like to express my appreciation to Florida Atlantic University's Division of Sponsored Research, which had enough confidence in the project to support it with a grant.

O. W. WILSON AND THE SEARCH FOR A POLICE PROFESSION

1

INTRODUCTION

In 1960, Orlando Winfield Wilson was appointed superintendent of police in Chicago in the wake of a police scandal which threatened to topple the administration of Mayor Richard Daley. Wilson, who was sixty years of age at the time, came from the University of California at Berkeley, where he had been dean of the School of Criminology.[1] The superintendency was described by one journalist as "one of the toughest of its kind in the world,"[2] and the dominant view of Chicagoans toward Wilson and his ability to succeed in office was probably reflected by a police captain who predicted, "he won't last six months."[3] Assuming control of an agency which a Cook County grand jury once described as "rotten to the core,"[4] in a city administered by one of the country's strongest and most controversial mayors, Wilson set out to reorganize the Chicago Police Department completely. Chicagoans looked on with cynicism molded by a century of intermittent police scandals.[5] Seven years later, on the eve of his sixty-seventh birthday, Wilson retired as superintendent, amidst an outpouring of public accolades and acclaim from the press unprecedented in Chicago police history. A local newspaper which had been a constant critic of the police department prior to Wilson editorialized upon his departure that, for the first time in its recollection, policemen "are now proud to serve."[6]

Orlando Wilson's seven-year tenure in Chicago was his most publicized professional venture. Yet, what Wilson accomplished in Chicago was simply a dramatic extension of what he had been doing and teaching for nearly a half-century. Wilson had been chief executive of three police departments during his career. His short-term influence on the affairs of those departments was significant; however, the long-term impact of

Wilson appeared to be transitory, as each agency was to eventually experience corruption in its ranks after he left.[7] Wilson's contribution to the police service cannot adequately be measured by his success in changing the direction of a single police department. Unlike colleagues, such as Los Angeles Chief of Police William H. Parker, Orlando Wilson's impact was on the institution of American law enforcement, rather than on a police department or departments in a single region of the country.

Orlando W. Wilson was a reformer. Wherever he went, change occurred, often too fast and too drastically to please those who supervised him, such as Wichita Mayor Robert E. Israel, who once angrily described Wilson as "too damned efficient."[8] He was a man who placed a high premium on loyalty. Nevertheless, his ultimate loyalty was not to the individual or agency which employed him, but to his rigid sense of ethics, and to the broad field of law enforcement, which he was convinced could become a profession. Contrary to the policies of competent chiefs of police elsewhere, who would identify, develop, promote, and encourage quality personnel to remain with their departments, Wilson would cultivate talented subordinates in hopes that they would eventually head police departments of their own. In essence, Wilson was deeply committed to upgrading law enforcement in general, as opposed to merely reforming an agency. As a chief of police Wilson would remain in office only when he was allowed to pursue a course of action in which loyalty to his department did not conflict with his commitment to police professionalization. However, when these dual loyalties did not coalesce, or when he could not faithfully serve a superior, Wilson would abandon his position, quietly, without recrimination. In any event, his belief in the need to professionalize law enforcement, decades before the idea became fashionable even among the police establishment, was to pervade his entire approach to public service.

Orlando Wilson was a person who commanded respect. He was a handsome man, tall, slender, erect, with steel grey hair parted and combed neatly to the side. He was a gifted public speaker with a resonant voice. During his years as superintendent of police in Chicago, Wilson's frequent press conferences impressed journalists with his ability to respond directly to the most penetrating questions.[9] A chain smoker, Wilson would usually face the press with hands clasped, a position which allowed him to conceal a hereditary tremor in his right hand. He was a stern man, aloof from all but his family and closest friends, to whom he was known as Winfield or "Win." Those who knew him casually or not at all referred to him as "O. W." Wilson was a private person. He kept his innermost thoughts and feelings to himself. Even during times of stress, he would refuse to openly criticize antagonists.[10] He studiously developed himself into a gentleman, a man of culture. Polite, distinguished, reserved to a point approaching haughtiness, Wilson had been raised to believe that the hallmarks of a gentleman were personal integrity, impeccable honesty, and dignity. As a consequence, Wilson never pandered to trifling emotions, such as petty jealousy.

O. W. Wilson was scrupulously honest, and he expected police officers, especially those who worked for him, to exhibit that same quality, to the extent that even the acceptance of a free cup of coffee should be a disciplinary offense.[11] He also felt strongly that a community had the right to require of its police department a maximum effort to fight crime and delinquency, to suppress vice, and to provide professional services. Despite his commitment to aggressive law enforcement, though, O. W. believed that the police had an obligation to "build good will and avoid resentment" in the community.[12]

Wilson was a martinet. He demanded from his personnel strict and unquestioned obedience to orders. Any breach of discipline, or the slightest departure from the lofty code of conduct he established, would be met with prompt disciplinary action. He had no patience with the incompetent, the dishonest, the corrupt, or the disloyal, and he swept these men aside with a ruthlessness that became a trademark.[13] It was to alienate even honest, competent police officers, and inhibit his ability to persuade them to voluntarily support his reform efforts.

Wilson had a penchant for orderliness which formed a basis for his conception of police professionalization. He believed that the affairs of a police department should be handled neatly, systematically, and with precision.[14] Thus, a primary concern of any police administrator should be to organize his department in some logical fashion—which to Wilson was along military lines. He unswervingly subscribed to the notions of narrow spans of control, a rigid chain of command, the sanctity of written policy pronouncements on a wide variety of subjects, specialization of tasks, carefully controlled delegations of authority and responsibility, and the close supervision of troops in the field. Wilson was convinced that a well-organized police department would instill pride in its officers. Corruption would be averted, and efficiency would become the rule when these principles of organization were supported with up-to-date tactical equipment, the scientific deployment of mobile, well-trained, college-educated troops, the installation of an advanced communications system, comprehensive records keeping, and an on-going public relations program. According to Wilsonian philosophy, a successful police venture would naturally result when a law enforcement agency committed to these principles was administered by a strong chief executive who ruled the department with an iron fist and was completely insulated from the intrusion of partisan politics. Within this framework, police officers would ultimately reach the pinnacle of professionalization by doing precisely what they were told to do by commanding officers. This view of professionalism has won widespread acceptance in law enforcement. It is narrow in the extreme, and has actually retarded professionalization by fostering an administrative attitude that rank and file police officers are not to be trusted: they must be closely watched, the subjects of massive policy pronouncements limiting their discretion, and consistently threatened with punishment to forestall misbehavior. It is ironic that a man who would contribute so much to the police professionalization movement would be the very one who would eventually preclude its success because of a cynical view of the human condition and a penchant for orderliness. He often became so preoccupied with mundane organizational matters that interpersonal relations both within and outside the departments he administered were neglected.

Wilson was born on a farm in Veblen, South Dakota, and raised in California by middle-class parents who never quite lost the folkways of their Norwegian forebears. The family was a patriarchy, ruled by Knute Vraalson, an attorney by training but a farmer and businessman by choice. In a home environment characterized by strict rules, young Wilson grew and was molded into manhood according to a rigid code of conduct.[15] He was expected to excel scholastically, embrace the Golden Rule, be a gentleman, seek a college education, and enter business. He fulfilled all expectations, save the last.

While pursuing a degree in engineering at the University of California at Berkeley, Wilson was forced to seek fulltime employment when his father suffered a business reversal. Accordingly, in 1921 he applied for and was appointed to a position as police officer with the Berkeley Police Department, administered by Chief August Vollmer, a major force in American law enforcement.[16] Vollmer saw great potential in young Wilson, and he encouraged him to stay in the police service. After Wilson received a degree in 1925, Chief Vollmer secured for his protégé the chief's job in Fullerton, a small city in southern California. Wilson was asked to resign within a year. His attempt to professionalize the police department was simply too radical for city officials.[17]

Bitter over his experience in Fullerton, O.W. Wilson drifted out of law enforcement until in 1928 August Vollmer again persuaded him to apply for a chief's position, this time in Wichita. He received the appointment and served in that capacity for eleven years. Wilson earned a reputation as an honest, innovative, creative administrator, somewhat atypical in the face of scandals of police corruption and inefficiency during Prohibition and the gangster era. In 1939, he was again asked to resign, this time by public officials who wished to reintroduce into Wichita the crimes and vice that Wilson had not permitted to flourish.[18]

That year, Wilson returned to the University of California as professor of police administration. He molded a fledgling degree program into a full School of Criminology and served as its first dean. Wilson remained in that capacity for twenty-one years, except for a tour of duty during World War II as director of de-Nazification activities in occupied Germany. Prior to his retirement in 1960, he defeated a move to have the School of Criminology abolished because it was too vocational.[19]

As he prepared to retire from the University of California, he received an urgent call from Chicago Mayor Richard Daley to chair a citizens committee empaneled to find a police commissioner. The former commissioner of police had resigned in the wake of the Summerdale Scandal, in which eight Chicago policemen were arrested for burglary. Unable to agree on a successor, the committee prevailed on Wilson to take the job, which he did, but only after receiving from Mayor Daley a three-year contract, assurances of complete support, and a pledge that the mayor would not interfere in the operations of the department. During Wilson's tenure in office, the Chicago Police Department became a model organization. Superintendent Wilson resigned in 1967, and returned to San Diego, where he spent his last years in relative seclusion.[20]

Orlando W. Wilson's public life was a struggle, a struggle to professionalize the police, often in the face of pressures to do otherwise. He was consistently thrust into situations in which he was forced to choose between the politically expedient road, which would have meant survival for him, and the morally correct path, which meant termination. Faced with that decision, he unhesitatingly chose the latter route.

Wilson's contributions to the field of law enforcement were immense: He was the Father of the Law Enforcement Code of Ethics; he inaugurated the first systematic approach to combatting juvenile delinquency; he began America's first police-college cadet program; he hired the first woman police captain; he pioneered state-sponsored training courses and minimum standards for police officers; he invented the idea of roll-call training, a compact period of instruction afforded officers before going on duty; he initiated psychological testing for selecting and promoting policemen; he conducted the first major statistical study of the deployment of patrol cars, from which he concluded that one-man cars were generally superior to two-man cars for general patrol work; he founded this country's first professional school of criminology; he authored the most widely circulated police administration textbook in history; he pioneered in adapting modern business records to police work, including computerization, records keeping, and communications systems. In addition,

Wilson placed hundreds of former students and subordinates in high-level police positions nationwide, and conducted reorganization studies of some forty police departments. O. W. Wilson's considerable accomplishments won the respect of his colleagues and the lasting enmity of FBI Director J. Edgar Hoover, whose thirty-year rivalry with Wilson led the envious director to use every opportunity to discredit his competitor.

Although it is possible to chronicle O. W. Wilson's technical innovations, his total impact cannot be quantitatively evaluated. Wilson represented a moral force, a phenomenon who molded men and ideas which were eventually to represent the mainstream of contemporary police thought. From Wichita, from Berkeley, and from Chicago he generated ideas and innovations; but mostly he produced men, men of the "Wilson School," who sought and received positions as teachers and police administrators nationwide. Moreover, many of those who did not fall directly under his tutelage were influenced by his writings.

In a very real sense, the public life of Orlando W. Wilson has implications for the entire field of law enforcement, for it deals with the political realities of police administration, the recurring problem of corruption, the often abrasive impact of reform, the nature of police-community relationships, the development of a police literature and opportunities for higher education, and with the fledgling professionalization movement. As law enforcement moves from a craft to a profession, and as institutions of higher learning continue to expand criminal justice coursework, students, policemen, and scholars are becoming increasingly aware of police history. The police professionalization movement is largely a search for status and identity, and a sense of history can furnish a foundation for the type of self-realization which is so essential to personal and professional development. It was not until the 1960's that the dream of professionalizing the police was transformed into a national movement. Orlando Wilson, more than any single figure, was responsible for this evolution. He did so with dogged persistence and a personal commitment to his sense of excellence. When he died in 1972, the International Association of Chiefs of Police published a full-page obituary which summarized his considerable contributions. In it, Wilson was described as the greatest authority on police administration that America had yet produced.[21]

2

YOUNG WINFIELD

Orlando W. Wilson's thinking was shaped, in large measure, by two extraordinary men. From August Vollmer he developed a public service ideal to which he would strictly adhere throughout his police career. From his father, however, Wilson inherited and was taught certain qualities which were to furnish a pattern for his life.

Ole Vraalson, Wilson's father, had a rather clearcut view of the human condition. To him, the difference between right and wrong was striking, and the grey areas of behavior existed only in the imagination of those concerned with excusing their failures or faults. A man could go about fulfilling his utmost potential only if he functioned as a gentleman in both his public dealings and private life. Vraalson's standards were high, his moral tone was lofty, and the code of conduct which he enforced on his children was strict and uncompromising; but he was a fair man, an individual of sensitivity and compassion.[1]

Ole was born in Norway in 1869. At an early age he emigrated to the United States with his parents. His mother was the daughter of a professor, and his father had been a farmer. The family settled in what is now Sedan, Minnesota, in an area populated by Scandinavian immigrant families. The Vraalsons homesteaded a small farm, which through hard work became quite productive.

Because of a modest financial success, the family was able to send Ole off to school. He received a B. A. from the University of Minnesota in 1890 and three years later earned his law degree. In an attempt to seek his fortune, young Vraalson set off for Spokane, where he entered private practice. His law practice did not flourish, however, partly due to the depression of 1893, and partly as a result of Ole's disinterest in the workaday life of an attorney. After two years, he returned to Minnesota. He invested what little money he had made in Spokane in a herd of mustang horses in Wyoming and Montana, which he planned to import to Minnesota as plow horses. He left this venture with a capital loss when he discovered that mustangs are not trainable for farm work.

In order to produce a stake, Vraalson persuaded his father to allow him to plant a bean crop on the family farm and keep the profits. This enterprise was successful, so that in 1896 young Ole relocated to Veblen, South Dakota, where he homesteaded a 160-acre farm and taught school. There he met and married a pretty young schoolteacher of Norwegian descent. Ole and Olava settled on the farm and raised "wheat, Flax and children." Three of the Vraalson's seven children were born in Veblen, including Orlando, who was born in 1900, and a younger sister who died in infancy.[2]

Ole Vraalson decided to change the family name to Wilson. Although he was not ashamed of his background, he believed that a career in business could be more lucratively pursued with an American name, for he had aspirations to invest what he made from the farm in other ventures. During the family's stay in Veblen, Ole entered politics, serving as county treasurer, and one term as a Populist state legislator.

In 1905, the Wilsons sold their holdings in South Dakota, moved their two children to Canada, and purchased a farm in Saskatchewan. Conditions were primitive; for the first two years the family lived in an abandoned railroad station. They eventually moved into a nearby town, from where the farm was run. Orlando Wilson, now called either Winfield or "Win" by his family and friends, entered school in Milestone, Saskatchewan.

Although Olava attended church regularly and the children went to Sunday school, the family was not particularly religious. The elder Wilson thought of himself as a Christian, but not one who needed the trappings of a formal religion in order to live a moral life. Olava and the children handled the religious enterprise, while he pursued the business of operating the farm. Ole Wilson practiced, preached, and lived the Protestant ethic. He was a confirmed capitalist; business, ethically practiced, was the noblest profession. This he impressed on the family, especially his eldest son, Orlando Winfield. He ordered his professional life around the related principles of self-discipline and work, initiative and acquisition, individualism and competition, principles which he tempered by a philosophy of honesty and openness in transactions and a commitment to obey the law in all cases. The cornerstone of his doctrine rested on the belief that every man is directly responsible for his life, and that he will eventually be held accountable for each action by a Supreme Being. By lecture and through example, Ole Wilson taught his son the value of a career in business, and to pursue it as a gentleman.

Consistent with the Wilson philosophy, each family member was expected to share in the work, though none of the children were assigned to backbreaking labor. Quite the contrary, the youngsters' work load was light and often more like play than labor. Orlando's primary task was to drive horse-drawn wagonloads of wheat into town at harvest time. He would arise early, hitch the team, assist in loading the wheat, and guide the wagon slowly toward town, until he was out of sight of the farm, at which time he would increase the team's speed from a walk to a frenzied gallop, at the risk of discipline upon fatherly detection.

Ole Wilson had high hopes for the future of his children, who despite the harsh Canadian environment, were expected to do well in school and develop their intellectual capabilities. Although the elder Wilson demanded that each child achieve his or her fullest potential, he was especially concerned with the progress of Winfield, in whom he recognized special intellectual qualities. But if young Wilson's father demanded extra work from his son, it was only because he knew Winfield was capable of producing it. Ole was strict and firm in his dealings with Orlando.[3]

As the farm became more and more productive, Ole Wilson invested the profits in grain elevators. Within a short time, he had purchased and constructed a sufficient number of elevators to make the farm an incidental business. In 1911, chiefly in reaction to the bitter Canadian winters, the family sold its farm and boarded a train for California. Locating in Anderson, in the midst of the Sacramento Valley, Wilson bought a parcel of land, subdivided it into building lots, then sold them at a profit. Two years later, Ole, now semiretired, secured a twenty-acre farm in Orland, California, and the family moved once again.[4]

The absence of a permanent home can have a negative impact on children who are forced to continuously relocate and attend a variety of public schools. But the Wilsons were a closeknit family, and the elder Wilson never permitted the moves to break down the strong relationships which had developed. The fact that the children were close did not mean that they were overly dependent on their parents or on one another. Ole Wilson would not have permitted this for an instant. Instead, the Wilson children, now six strong, were expected to assert their independence. It was during an early quest for independence that young Wilson was seriously injured.

When twelve-year old Winfield asked his parents to go deer hunting by bicycle in the rugged stretches of northern California, they agreed, but not without some reservations. Although the soft-spoken boy had exhibited maturity beyond his years, the dangerousness of such an undertaking could not be denied. Still, the Wilsons had not the slightest intention of coddling the young man for whom they had such high hopes of future success. Consequently, laden with camping equipment, the youngster bravely pedaled off on his adventure. Unfortunately, the trip was curtailed when, at the height of the hunt, Orlando fell from his bicycle and badly fractured his left arm.[5]

The boy's recuperative period was long and painful. As a result of the injury his left arm would not fully develop, and he would grow to manhood with it one and one-half inches shorter than the right. It also forcefully curtailed whatever interest he had in sports, to the delight of his father, who viewed sports as a counterproductive and ungentlemanly type of activity at best.[6] Though Orlando had always been a good student, during this prolonged period of recovery he refined his study habits to a point of scholarship which pleased his parents. Wilson later described this experience:

> During my period of convalescence I developed a certain sedateness and studiousness out of keeping with my years, which condition was aggravated by our removal to San Diego, where I was not acquainted and, due to a natural shyness—which, by the way I have largely conquered—I took no interest in anything but my books.[7]

In the midst of his recuperation, the family moved once again, this time to southern California. The elder Wilson built a beach house in Pacific Beach, a suburb of San Diego, then constructed a large home in San Diego, at the edge of Balboa Park. The home was a rambling, comfortable two-story frame structure which the children, long after they had grown to adulthood, would affectionately refer to as "the big house."[8] A major section of the house was set aside for young Wilson. He had a private bedroom, the almost exclusive use of a darkroom in which to practice a short-lived photographic hobby, and a private office connected to his bedroom. Ole Wilson expected his son to excel scholastically, so he felt it only appropriate that he provide the resources Orlando Winfield needed to produce results. With these advantages, Winfield's failure to achieve academic excellence would have brought a harsh response from his father. Young Wilson never let the patriarch down.

Ole Wilson insisted that certain customs be observed by all. Meals, for example, were formal ceremonies. Everyone was punctual, table manners were strictly enforced, and members dressed for every meal. There were no robes or pajamas at the breakfast table, and dinner meant ties for the boys and dresses for the girls. Father, of course, presided at the head of the table, leading what conversation there was, inquiring into the state of each child's schoolwork. If he detected any academic deficiencies, the offender could expect a stern lecture and some personal guidance with homework.[9] O. W. Wilson stood in awe of his father, and was deferential toward him.

During O. W.'s adolescence, progressivism was at its height in California. Reformer Hiram Johnson was governor, and muckraking journalists were filling periodicals and newspapers with articles on governmental and business corruption. Ole Wilson read his newspapers from cover to cover. He was appalled at the apparent moral and ethical breakdown in society, as men in positions of responsibility consistently betrayed their trusts. It was ungentlemanly and completely unacceptable behavior. To Winfield, the message was regularly brought home: "Don't do anything which will get your name in the newspapers."[10] In short, the father was telling his son that he should not do anything which he would be ashamed to have the community find out about.

Ole Wilson neither drank, nor smoked, nor gambled; and he did not completely approve of those who did, especially if they did so in excess. Thus far, there had been no need to impress this on O. W. But an incident occurred when Orlando was in high school which gave his father an opportunity to provide additional training in moral values. Orlando had developed an interest in statistics in a high school mathematics course. As a consequence, he decided that he would make his new-found knowledge work for him by creating a system which would break the bank in a Tijuana gambling casino. He assigned his brothers to roll dice for the better part of three days while he calculated the probability of odds on each number. During the height of the experiment, Ole Wilson, suspicious over the long periods of silence, inspected the bedroom area, where he discovered his sons shooting dice. Disapproving, but satisfied by O. W.'s explanation, the patriarch told his eldest son that he would fund the experiment by furnishing him with one hundred dollars to test his system. Elated, Orlando took the money and left for Tijuana early one Saturday morning. He returned that evening, penniless and better off for his experience. Almost fifty years later, O. W. Wilson and his wife were vacationing at Lake Tahoe, when they entered a gambling casino. Wilson strode to a roulette table, and placed a dime on a number. The croupier promptly informed him that the game had a twenty-five cent limit, whereupon Orlando Winfield Wilson took his dime and withdrew.[11]

Through his junior year in high school, young Orlando had made no firm vocational choice. His father had been meticulously guiding him toward a career in business, but not into any particular field. In the summer before his senior year at San Diego High School, however, O. W. selected a career. Some years before, Ole Wilson had purchased a northern California gold mine, which produced just enough ore to keep it open.

Orlando decided to spend his summer there, exploring the countryside, inspecting the sprawling mine shafts. He left, characteristically alone, by train. His father shipped a motorcycle to the mine for transportation. O. W. slept in the miners' bunkhouse, a twenty- by fifty-foot barracks. He ate with the workers and interrogated the mine manager about mineralogy, geology, and the various fields of engineering. At summer's end, he drove his Scout motorcycle leisurely back to San Diego with a career goal: mining engineering.

As a high school senior, Wilson took part in several student activities. He had a small role in the senior class play and served on the debate team. Like most teenagers, Orlando was given a nickname by his classmates, who called him "Windy," partly a contraction of his middle name, but primarily because of his economy of conversation.[12] In 1918, Orlando Winfield Wilson graduated from San Diego High School at the head of his class. He was selected to deliver the valedictory address. No one could have been prouder or less surprised than Ole Wilson.

At eighteen years of age, Orlando Wilson had grown to manhood. He was tall and slender, possessor of wisdom which belied his years. To the family, Wilson's eventual success was a *fait accompli*. He would go away to the University of California at Berkeley to major in civil engineering, an education which would be completely financed by his father. His future was bright, and all but assured. Yet, the frailties of the human condition often dictate modifications in the firmest of plans. Orlando would attend the University of California, but his ultimate success would be in a field to which he had thus far given no consideration.

As he left for the university, he was exceptionally well prepared to excel, being a scholar of unquestioned ability. Insofar as his personal qualities were concerned, he was his father's son. Ole Wilson had molded Winfield into precisely the type of person the patriarch admired. To sum up the whole of a human personality in a few sentences is a venture fraught with peril, but it is safe to say that young Wilson exhibited certain clearly identifiable personal characteristics which had been purposefully transmitted to him by his father. Furthermore, throughout his lifetime, Wilson's faith in the correctness of the personal traits which he had accumulated through childhood was never shaken.

O. W. Wilson had been taught to be frugal, soft-spoken, courteous, respectful of people in authority, well-disciplined, independent, hard working, scholarly, and competitive. The fabric of his philosophy was woven around the idea that a true gentleman is one who pursues his calling, whatever it may be, with unswerving honesty—meaning that a man is only as good as the personal integrity he maintains. Stealing, then, is not only illegal and immoral, it is undignified behavior, beneath the level at which a gentleman should operate. O. W., like his father, had a clear, uncluttered sense of what constituted right and wrong. Unlike the Wilson patriarch, however, Orlando held no prudish view of smoking, drinking, and gambling, which in fact he more than tolerated. Nevertheless, the implications for Wilson's later police service are clear. He would never involve himself in any activity which would adversely affect his stature as a gentleman.

Unfortunately, despite his considerable accomplishments, Orlando Wilson was also an unwitting victim of his greatest virtues, a "black letter guy" who saw the rules of life in the same way an attorney reads the main chapter headings in a law book, and nothing more.[13] His rules were *the* rules, and wherever he went he demanded strict adherence. Unquestionably, his personal code of conduct was impeccable, beyond reproach. But in a society composed of strong men, weak men, and men who make mistakes, surely there is room for errors in judgment and excusable personal frailties. Yet O. W. Wilson was to see all forms of venal corruption as a malignancy needing radical surgery. Consequently, his methods in dealing with police corruption and suspected corruption were often heavy-handed. Notwithstanding the inarguable morality of his position and his sincerity of purpose, the lack of empathy he often displayed for the officers who labored at the lowest levels of law enforcement was to mar his career.

O. W. Wilson's sense of loyalty was a trait developed early in life. He was constantly taught that persons in positions of authority deserved unquestioned respect and obedience. His father both expected and demanded deference. As a result, Wilson viewed authority figures with a respect bordering on awe. He would consistently, and without question, obey orders from higher authority, except cases in which they ran contrary to his values. Wilson felt that if he could not in good conscience obey an order from his superior, his recourse was not to resist or to argue, but to resign, quietly and with dignity. He expected people who worked for him to display the same deference, an expectation which was not always fulfilled.

3

COLLEGE COP

Orlando Winfield Wilson went away to the University of California in the fall of 1919. He had made firm career plans to be a mining engineer, and his studies were designed to help him meet that objective. Orlando found temporary quarters in a student rooming house, but later moved to a partially furnished studio apartment in a private home at 1118 Laurel Street in Berkeley. The apartment had been converted from a bedroom by the landlord, and consisted of a parlor, a closet, and a private bath. A couch served as his bed, and he studied at a small table. Wilson called the apartment his "island," and he dutifully sent home to the family a minutely detailed diagram of it. By living alone, he had once again asserted his independence. The door had a fine new lock, to which he was entrusted with a key. He confided to his sister that:

> The door has a Yale lock and I am the proud possessor of a latch key, and it gives me a very special feeling when I let myself in for an evening.[1]

Young Wilson cheerfully immersed himself in schoolwork. Most of the engineering courses were combined lectures and laboratory assignments, so that there was little correlation between credit hours and actual time expended. In one week, a three-semester-hour course in mining engineering often entailed three class lecture hours, five hours in the mineralogy laboratory, and five or more hours of outside readings. Young O. W. reported to his father that four days of the week he began his school day at eight A.M. and finished at four P.M. "with one hour off for lunch."[2]

The engineering majors with whom Wilson studied were an older group than those in other degree programs. Many were World War I veterans;

some had even worked as miners and were familiar with, as Orlando put it, the "smell of burned powder and the clatter of drills." He was quite impressed with them, especially their dedication to hard work and long hours of study. In one letter he boasted that engineering students unflaggingly worked twelve to fourteen hours a day in order to get everything they could from their courses, while Letters and Arts students constantly recoiled at having to devote more time to a course than its credit hour value. He once described his engineering colleagues as:

> Mighty fine fellows . . . the kind who will stick to a pal. Friendship means more to them than merely a speaking acquaintance. They are real men . . . they put in from 12 to 14 hours of hard work each day, and it keeps a person humping to keep up with them, because as a rule they are older students, and are no slouches when it comes to grey matter.[3]

Despite his derision of Letters and Arts students, O. W. Wilson had a high regard for the liberal arts. On a number of occasions he wrote to his family of the need for a gentleman to be broadly educated so that he could become cultured. He was encouraged to pursue cultural interests by the engineering faculty, who thought that engineers should be looked up to by American society, as they were in Europe. European engineers were forced to gain an understanding of broad cultural matters, and Berkeley's engineering faculty often assigned their students to take elective work in the social and behavioral sciences, and in the humanities.

Of all the faculty members Wilson admired, he had a special feeling for his dean, whom he saw as a cultured gentleman. Of the dean, O. W. once wrote:

> He is a cultured man, quite the gentleman under all conditions, and he tries to impress us with this quality . . . the American engineer, according to the dean, is always a gentleman, but too often a diamond in the rough, utterly lacking in the finer polish of culture.[4]

O. W. Wilson decided that he would not lack this "finer polish of culture" so he pursued his instinct and this professorial advice by taking courses in English, literature, economics, social science, history, political science, and philosophy.

Since Orlando Wilson's sense of preparing to be a gentleman meant more than merely academic preparation, he set out to mold himself toward that end in other ways. Wilson detected in himself what he thought was a serious flaw, indeed a debilitating one in terms of becoming a person worthy of the term *gentleman*. He exhibited a certain shyness, which he diagnosed as a "fear of people."[5] Accordingly, he had studiously avoided crowds and social events. Moreover, young Winfield had never found the time to foster any sort of close relationship with girls, except his mother and sisters. In truth, he was quite inexperienced in this regard, preferring his books over social relationships. It took university life to point up this void in his life, but when O. W. became aware of it he took remedial action.

Wilson began attending dances, plays, parties, lectures, concerts, and various types of social gatherings, often in the company of girls, a previously rare sight. He originally intended this venture to be an intellectually broadening experience, and he undertook it in as systematic a way as a doctor would embark on corrective surgery. But he was delighted to discover that his interest in girls and social life transcended mere intellectual experience. He liked girls, and they, it seemed, liked him.[6] As Wilson became increasingly active socially, he began to lose that shyness which had long characterized him. Orlando Winfield was never to become an open, gregarious, life-of-the-party type. He would eventually be able to function adequately in any group environment, though inside he did not always feel completely comfortable with strangers.

As O. W. Wilson became more and more involved in university life, he began to develop those intellectual and interpersonal skills so necessary to professional success. His attitude toward the role of ladies and gentlemen in society became quite fixed, and can be best seen in the way in which he responded to a personal situation involving a younger sister, Lyla. In one of her letters, Lyla Wilson had expressed an interest in seeking employment in a dance hall. Winfield was sincerely shocked. He wrote back that college graduates felt dance halls were "low brow," and that public opinion would condemn her for entering such a "tough joint."[7] He urged her to develop "refinement," which he described in some depth:

> Don't allow yourself to become coarse. I am not speaking of the mental or the moral now, only of the physical. Develop refinement— charm, personality. Consider the voice, learn to modulate it, to speak only in pleasing tones. Never allow it to become harsh or shrill even when angry. Always keep it under control and make it pleasing to the ear—calm and quiet—not shrill, harsh and loud. And there is your general physical carriage . . . walk with grace.[8]

It was during this series of letters to Lyla Wilson that Winfield articulated a philosophy of life, to which he commended her. Wilson entitled it "the Law of Consideration," and it fairly represented an inner postulate which would consistently characterize his standard of behavior. According to this law, a person should, early in life, develop a personal or career objective to which he would aspire. This ultimate object should be a lofty one. Once it had been formalized, everything that the person did should in some way be related to the achievement of that end, whatever it was. Thus, an individual would act out of "consideration" for the life role he had chosen for himself. As a gentleman, he would order his life around this "Law of Consideration."

On transacting with other people Wilson, in a letter to Lyla, further describes his "Law of Consideration":

> There is one trait in your moral makeup which you must build up; and that is consideration . . . be considerate, consider the other person's feelings and never hurt them . . . consideration is the basis of personality . . . never be guilty of doing or saying a mean thing about anybody. If you can't say anything nice about a person, don't say anything.[9]

Wilson had never developed an interest in sports, or had a long-lasting hobby, or worked out of a need to do so, except for chores on the family's farm. Almost every waking hour since childhood had been spent accumulating knowledge. In essence, the development of O. W. Wilson into a quality person had been his only real fulltime undertaking. He took himself quite seriously, not in a narcissistic or self-indulgent way, but with the belief that each person has certain capabilities which, if developed, can lead to a fruitful and productive life. Consequently, this personal development took all forms: intellectual, social, behavioral, ethical. Even hygiene played a part, as he counseled Lyla to "take a bath—two or three times a week—and keep your nails scrupulously clean."[10] But above all, one must "be honest but above all be honest to your self. The most dangerous liar in the world is one who lies to himself."[11]

O. W. Wilson was to practice these rules during his life. In those situations in which lesser men would have lashed out at critics or detractors, he stood silent, even as he was being castigated by others. Wilson's private philosophy and public behavior remained consistent throughout his lifetime.

Wilson felt that the pursuit of pleasure was counterproductive in the life of one who had an obligation to excel. He counselled Lyla to forsake momentary enjoyment, and in so doing spoke of his destiny, as he saw it:

> I would say at once—by all means go and get from life what little enjoyment it holds for you. But you are capable of better things— someday we will all be on top, and it is that day I am looking forward to. And so I would say, act accordingly.[12]

During his early university years, O. W. often amused himself by writing poetry, usually on notebook paper. He destroyed some poems, but many of them were sent home. His normal handwriting was excellent; flowing graceful, elegant. But he seemed to take extra care with his handwriting when transcribing his poetry, and the product often took on a scroll-like quality. A brief excerpt from an untitled verse follows:

> The sun has disappeared behind a glowing cloud
> we speak in cautious whispers
> we dare not speak aloud
> we sit in silent wonder, our faces to the west
> and I look with awe and silence on
> that which is our best
> we wonder and we are puzzled by what we see
> the piled up stratum, pink and green, from zenith to the sea.

Orlando was happy in school. His studies were difficult, but he dedicated himself, allocated his time systematically, and was a true scholar. He liked his fellow students and admired most of the faculty, especially those who had actual field experience in addition to academic credentials. Still, he began to have misgivings about the correctness of his decision to embark on a career in mining engineering. There was an opportunity to become financially well-off in mining, but Wilson, although interested in financial gain, did not believe it should be the determining factor in the selection of a career. He was simply not sure that engineering would satisfy him intellectually. To pursue a calling only for money would be unthinkable because, according to O. W., "for a man who follows a profession merely for the livelihood he gains, life is scarcely worth living."[13] As the young man became exposed to coursework outside the College of Engineering, he came to deeply question the wisdom of his present vocational plans. Wilson had taken liberal arts courses, and had spent a summer in the Reserve Officers' Training Corps (ROTC). As a consequence, he began casting about for a career which would allow him to use the knowledge he had acquired in courses in political science, anthropology, genetics, ethics, and psychology in a leadership capacity of some sort. He had been appointed as student squad leader in the ROTC, and he enjoyed commanding men.[14] He thought that he might be able to fulfill this new-found leadership aspiration by entering mine management rather than engineering.[15] However, before he could arrive at a final decision in the matter, fate took a hand in the form of a family crisis, making his deliberations moot. As a result, O. W. was thrust into a career which would furnish an outlet for all his personal needs and professional ambitions.

During World War I, Ole Wilson had purchased extensive acreage in the Imperial Valley. He had hoped to hold the land, much of it farmland, until it inflated in value, then sell at a profit. Unfortunately, the end of World War I was followed by a recession. His investment had disastrous consequences, and financially the Wilson patriarch found himself in dire economic straits.[16] Since Winfield's education was being completely financed by his father, the ripples of the setback were felt all the way to Berkeley.

Orlando had some money, and Ole offered to send him a little more, but it was clear that if young Wilson wished to continue his education beyond that school year he would have to find a way to become financially self-sufficient. O. W. at first considered dropping out of school, but that possibility was eliminated. Instead, he decided to look for a job.

In the spring of 1921 Wilson saw an advertisement in the university newspaper announcing examinations for police patrolmen in Berkeley and inviting students to apply. Wilson thought it odd that the police department wanted students in their ranks, but due to his crisis he did not intend to question any prospective employer's motives. O. W. reported on the posted date, and along with approximately fifty other hopefuls, filed into the Berkeley High School assembly room for testing. It was there that he was to first meet Chief August Vollmer, who told the assemblage that they were to be given the Army Alpha Test, a general intelligence examination. Applicants who scored high would then enter the second stage of testing, the physical examination.[17]

O. W. Wilson passed the Alpha Test, and was ranked at the top of his group. He underwent a physical examination with Dr. John Rowell, who also questioned him closely to determine if he had any emotional disorders. Wilson was impressed. A written test, a physical examination, and a psychological evaluation, all to become a simple policeman, were more hurdles than he had expected to encounter. Wilson survived this phase, and he progressed to the last obstacle, an interview with August Vollmer.[18]

The Berkeley Police Department was located in the basement of City Hall. Chief Vollmer's office was small and sparsely furnished with a desk, several wooden chairs, and a file cabinet. When subordinates came to see the chief he expected their visits to be brief. O. W. Wilson's interview was likewise brief; less than five minutes. There is no record of the conversation, but it must have gone well, for Wilson was immediately hired. He was told that he would need a car. The police department had no vehicles. Moreover, he had to purchase from a local hardware store a .38 caliber Smith and Wesson Police Special revolver and a billy club. The uniform also had to be purchased by recruits.[19] O. W. took what money he had and invested it in the required equipment. The car, a Model T Ford touring car, was purchased with the minimum down payment allowable. Wilson was sworn in and readied for work.

When O. W. Wilson entered the police service in 1921, the state of law enforcement nationwide was generally dismal. Exposés of graft and corruption were widespread. Inefficiency was the rule rather than the exception, while policemen were largely untrained, uneducated, ill-equipped, and badly paid.[20] Law enforcement in Berkeley differed dramatically from that found in other cities. With a population of approximately 25,000 residents it had no serious crime problem, although pickpockets, small-time burglars, petty thieves, and bootleggers did ply their trades there. Policemen, however, found that a great deal of their time was spent enforcing minor violations of the law perpetrated by students at the University of California. For their work, officers were well-paid, well-trained and educated, and freed from the influence of partisan politics, thanks to August Vollmer.

August Vollmer was to play an important role in Orlando Wilson's life, both personally and professionally. Vollmer was described by his biographer as having contributed as much toward police science "as any man who ever lived."[21] He had been elected marshal of Berkeley in 1905, and when the position was made appointive, he was selected as chief of police, a post he held until 1932. During his early years at Berkeley, Vollmer was the first police official to utilize the polygraph; he invented a record-keeping system which became a model; he developed a *modus operandi* (M. O.) file which catalogued the techniques of robbers and burglars to facilitate later apprehensions; he pioneered psychological examinations for police candidates, introduced two-way radios into police cars, wrote the nation's first definitive text on police administration, and pioneered juvenile delinquency prevention programs. As Vollmer's reputation grew, he began to receive requests from public officials across the country to study their police departments and make recommendations for improvements. Thus, "the chief," as he was called by almost everyone, became America's first police management consultant. During his career, he consulted with approximately two hundred law enforcement agencies. Moreover, he was responsible for the creation of the first police education program at a university, and spent his entire career encouraging other universities to do the same. His encouragement of college-educated officers to seek careers with the Berkeley Police Department was another groundbreaking innovation. His university-educated officers were later to earn the affectionate title of "college cops" by both colleagues and the community.[22]

When O. W. Wilson entered the police service in Berkeley, Chief August

COLLEGE COP / 23

Vollmer was just reaching a position of preeminence in law enforcement. This was to affect Wilson's eventual career, for without the chief's assistance, O. W. would not have been permitted to seek his destiny so early in life, and to move upward at such a steady pace. But Vollmer recognized in Wilson certain qualities which were critically needed in law enforcement, even before young Wilson recognized them in himself. While Orlando pursued what he thought was a part-time job, Chief Vollmer had identified him for much greater things.

Before he was released on his own beat, O. W. Wilson received the customary training: a briefing from the chief, a tour of the police station, and a one-week break-in period with a veteran officer. He was then assigned to patrol duty on the 4:00 P.M. to midnight shift in north Berkeley. His patrol car had no red light or siren, no radio, and no distinctive markings. It was, to Wilson, a new experience, one with which he was completely unfamiliar, but from which he received a great deal of satisfaction.[23]

All Berkeley police officers received for their labors $140 monthly, with uniformed patrolmen alloted an extra $30 as a car allowance. For this, they worked an eight-hour day, six days per week. Overtime was frequent and unpaid, and since an officer's daily reports were prepared after the completion of his tour of duty, it was a fortunate patrolman indeed who could keep his day's work from extending beyond nine hours. Off-duty court appearances were simply one's "contribution," and if a University of California football game, or other event calling for crowd control, occurred on an officer's day off, he would have to work. Because of the frequency with which the university scheduled special events, it was not unusual to find the entire forty-man department on duty at once. As a consequence, O. W. lessened his normal academic load from eighteen semester hours to twelve or less.[24] It was one of the prices that an individual paid for financial independence.

Wilson was one of Chief Vollmer's first "college cops." A former University of California football star, Walter Gordon, had led the way the previous year. Gordon was quickly accepted by his colleagues, for they were flattered to have a celebrity working in their midst. Other student-officers were viewed with skepticism at first, especially by those patrolmen who had no college training and who were concerned about competing for promotion with those who did. There was never outright hostility directed at the new officers. The initial posture of veterans was aloofness. They were wary of relying on young men who might not be equipped to cope with the rigors of police work. Officer O. W. Wilson did much to allay this initial suspicion.

August Vollmer's biographer tells a story about Wilson's early police career, which has been confirmed by William Dean, a former Berkeley policeman. Frank Waterbury was a veteran Berkeley officer whose attitude symbolized the prevailing early outlook of "old-timers" toward "college cops." One day, during one of O. W.'s first tours of duty, Waterbury sought out Chief Vollmer and said: "I've changed my mind about these college kids." When Vollmer asked why, Waterbury replied:

> You know Wilson, your college recruit? He came in last evening with Kid Bennet, that escaped convict, and you know he's one of the toughest thugs we've had in a long time. Wilson got both of the Kid's guns and had him handcuffed. I asked Wilson how he did it and he said he followed this suspicious-looking man and saw him trying to break into a house. Now what do you think this college cop does? He proceeds to tell Bennet that if he makes one move, it will be his last.[25]

Waterbury had been converted to the Vollmer philosophy, and Wilson and his colleagues were eventually accepted into the veterans' ranks.

Since the patrol cars had no radio communication equipment, Chief Vollmer installed a Gamewell light system in the city, red lights strategically placed in prominent places throughout Berkeley. The lights would be activated by the desk sergeant in police headquarters if an officer was needed to answer a call. When a patrolman saw this signal, it was his job to immediately report to the nearest call box and call in for instructions. Young O. W. was consistently the first one to call in and arrive at crime scenes, as he gained a reputation for aggressiveness and competitiveness on the beat.[26]

Even the toughest veterans began to admire O. W. Wilson. He was always "on his call," never asked special favors, did not flaunt his education, and often volunteered for work that others tried to avoid. For example, he unhesitatingly accepted an assignment to inspect fraternity houses on campus to see if the students had stolen city equipment to display on the walls. The job won him no friends among the student body, and was described by Wilson in the following way:

> I have to go into every backyard and inspect the sanitary conditions, and into every frat house and take away all their booty—signs, lanterns, etc., that they have picked up in their more frivolous moments. I have an opportunity of raking down a few enemies. But a police officer is expected to have a lot of those, especially in the rougher parts of town, where everyone hates the sight of a cop. But such are the trials and tribulations of the profession.[27]

Patrolman Wilson began to earn a reputation as a "black letter man" even at this early date. His devotion to duty, the precise way in which he prepared reports, his obedience to orders, all contributed to this reputation. Moreover, his serious, almost stern exterior, convinced many of his colleagues that he was totally dedicated to the pursuit of pure police work.[28] Certainly no one could have questioned his dedication, but as in later life his sternness was more apparent than real. He had a sense of humor, though it only occasionally broke to the surface. Once, Wilson and another officer were dispatched to pick up a suicide victim in north Berkeley and deliver him to the morgue; there were no medical examiner wagons at the time. O. W. propped the corpse up in a sitting position in the back seat of his Model T Ford and drove into the center of town with the other patrolman beside the deceased. When they encountered an officer on traffic duty, he was summoned to the car to meet a "distinguished observer." Wilson's partner extended the corpse's hand in greeting, the officer grasped it, recoiling as he discovered what had happened. The two patrol officers drove off laughing in the night. The grisly incident was not typical of O. W., yet he was capable of injecting humor into any situation, although usually in a more subtle way.

O. W. Wilson was not a man to let a criminal offender free. Accordingly, he spent a great deal of his off-duty time in court. The Alameda County District Attorney's Office had assigned a prosecutor to Berkeley— a bright, young, aggressive attorney named Earl Warren. Warren and Wilson struck up a quick friendship. O. W. was impressed with the energetic way with which Warren prosecuted his adversaries, and the time he devoted to helping Berkeley policemen prepare their criminal cases. Even after they parted company in 1925, Wilson proudly kept track of Warren's career, from the district attorney's office to the governor's mansion, and eventually to the United States Supreme Court. When Warren did ascend to the high court, Wilson was aghast at the apparent reversal of his philosophy of a lifetime. To O. W. Wilson, the Earl Warren court overstepped the limits of reason and logic in releasing convicted criminals on legal technicalities. It was to be one of Wilson's unhappiest memories, and he would never forgive Earl Warren for his treachery.

Yet, O. W. Wilson, who had never been accused of being soft on crime, once released an obviously guilty offender with a warning. In 1921, during "big game" week at the University of California, O. W. was on traffic duty when he stopped a traffic violator for speeding. The driver was a beautiful, dark-haired young French major named Vernis Haddon. They struck up a conversation, and he found that she had recently transferred to Berkeley from the University of Texas after her socially prominent family had moved from Houston to Los Angeles. She was also an intercollegiate swimmer and diver. Vernis had an effervescent, outgoing personality which often overwhelmed a young man. O. W. Wilson was overwhelmed. To Vernis, O. W. was a refreshing change from the men with whom she had been keeping company. He was neither frivolous nor polished. Instead, Wilson was studious, bright, and thoughtful. He was a gentleman, without the foppish qualities of the upperclassmen who populated Berkeley's fraternity houses. Six weeks after they met young Wilson made an uncharacteristically impulsive decision when he eloped to Sacramento with Vernis.[29]

The Wilsons moved into a small studio apartment on Durant Avenue. Since Orlando worked from 4:00 P.M. to midnight and attended classes in the mornings, the opportunity for a social life all but escaped the newlyweds. Still, Vernis was an inventive girl who liked to socialize, so those precious free moments were often devoted to the pursuit of restrained pleasure. The apartment was located in a quiet residential neighborhood. Parties and postmidnight noise-making of any kind were prohibited. A weekly pancake supper or a late ride with friends often constituted their social life, with the exceptions of an occasional play or a sporting event. Vernis, however, would not allow Orlando's job to completely interfere with social activities. She even hit upon a way to create out of her husband's position a social opportunity.

Officer Wilson and a colleague, patrolman William Dean,[30] had been selected by Chief Vollmer for an undercover assignment, partly because of their service record, and partly because they appeared too young to be policemen. It was during the height of Prohibition, and the officers were ordered to infiltrate restaurants to determine if they were dealing in illicit alcohol. Vernis decided that the project had a better chance of success if the two young men brought dates along. Vernis, of course, was Orlando's date, while Lucrezia Denton, a close friend, would accompany Dean.[31] For weeks they combined business with pleasure, but not to the point that Wilson overlooked the objective of his assignment. The officers were extraordinarily successful at their task; so successful in fact that news of their accomplishments in convicting Prohibition violators spread to other communities. The marshal of Albany, a neighboring town, asked Chief Vollmer to loan him the services of this highly successful enforcement team. Vollmer consented, and Wilson and Dean were able to assemble enough evidence to convict a restaurant owner whom the marshal had been after for months.[32]

With the increased demands made on O. W. by his job and his new marriage, Wilson's studies began to suffer. Although he seriously contemplated leaving school until Ole Wilson had recouped his financial losses, he decided against that move. O. W. was bothered by the fact that his brothers and sisters had all gone to work, and he was the only one in college. But, his decision to stay in school was based upon the fact that he was now economically self-sufficient, no longer a drain on the family. Furthermore, if he was ever to be in a position to help his father, he would be hardpressed to do so without a degree.[33]

In 1923 a massive fire swept north Berkeley, leaving hundreds homeless and threatening scores of homes and businesses. All days off were cancelled, and officers were assigned to sixteen-hour shifts for almost a month in order to assist fire victims. On one occasion, Wilson helped a beleaguered professor roll his beloved piano down Euclid Avenue, a not inconsiderable project. On another, O. W. was assigned to a traffic post when someone stole his police car. A subsequent search turned up the vehicle, and it was returned intact to the embarrassed patrolman. Later, Chief Vollmer received a letter from an anonymous citizen thanking him for the "loan" of the car, which was used to evacuate prized possessions from the fire. That semester, O. W. Wilson flunked out of the university. He was readmitted the following term, changed his major to economics, and resumed his studies.[34]

Orlando Wilson enjoyed his work, though he never seriously considered it as a career, at least not in the early days. Yet, August Vollmer had identified in the young patrolman leadership capabilities which he believed would make him a valuable addition to law enforcement. Vollmer was not one to allow a good man to escape to another profession without a fight. Every facet of Wilson's performance as a Berkeley police officer had been superlative. He was honest, dedicated, an aggressive patrolman, a tenacious investigator, and courteous in his dealing with citizens. Furthermore, Officer Wilson exhibited a talent which Vollmer admired in his men, but rarely encountered: the ability to write well. The chief constantly encouraged policemen "who knew anything to put it down on paper."[35] Daily, he would review the case reports completed by his men during the preceding tours of duty. Wilson's reports were precise, accurate, and impeccably typed. Chief Vollmer tried to impress on all his officers the importance of writing about their police experience, in order to contribute to the growing fund of law enforcement literature. Of all Vollmer's men, O. W. came in for special attention. Vollmer was eventually to persuade Wilson to publish a book on police administration, albeit twenty years later.

August Vollmer was clearly interested in preparing Wilson for an eventual leadership position in law enforcement, and he made use of every opportunity to guide O. W. toward that end. The chief and his premier patrolman later became close friends, but never as long as Wilson was a Berkeley police officer. Vollmer had a rather firm view of the formal relationship that should exist between superiors and subordinates. August Vollmer was the chief and O. W. Wilson was a patrolman. To tinker with that arrangement could, in Vollmer's view, upset departmental morale and discipline, while exposing him to charges of favoritism. Nevertheless, Vollmer allowed himself to cement a closer relationship with Wilson than he had with other subordinates, within, of course, acceptable limits.[36]

To Vollmer, the police department was a human laboratory, a training ground. Officers were constantly upgrading their knowledge and skills under his direction. He would take policemen on tours of prisons and mental institutions, conduct training seminars, and hold weekly "crab meetings," usually on Friday afternoons. A "crab meeting" was an assembly of off-duty officers to which Vollmer would invite experts in various scientific fields to discuss their specialties. In so doing, the chief was able to point out the uses of science in crime detection. One Friday, a phrenologist, who maintained that he could tell a man's character by the bumps on his head, was invited to lecture officers. At the end of his talk, Chief Vollmer offered to produce a prisoner for a demonstration. The phrenologist accepted, and a shabbily dressed policeman in the guise of a prisoner presented himself for examination. The phrenologist labeled him a confirmed criminal with no hope for rehabilitation. The message Vollmer had given was clear: science had value to policemen, but it had limitations as well.

Wilson neither saw his chief socially, nor was he ever invited to August Vollmer's office to sit and talk, because of Vollmer's feelings on fraternizing. He did find other ways to counsel O. W. within the acceptable framework of their formal superior-subordinate relationship. Chief Vollmer had never learned to drive. When he needed a driver, an available patrolman would ordinarily be selected. More often than not, O. W. Wilson was that patrolman. He would drive the chief to his destination, with Vollmer ceremoniously placed in the back seat of Wilson's Model T. Enroute, they would have brief conversations about O. W.'s plans to someday enter business, and Vollmer's hope that he would not. The two men came to know each other quite well during these discussions, and their mutual respect grew.

In the fall of 1925, Orlando W. Wilson received his baccalaureate degree from the University of California. To Wilson, his career as a police officer was drawing to a close as he cast about for a position in business. Chief Vollmer, however, was not willing to let his young protégé desert law enforcement. Officials from Fullerton, a small southern California city, had asked Vollmer to recommend a candidate for chief of police. Although O. W. Wilson had but four years police experience, and had never commanded men except in the ROTC, Vollmer immediately thought of him for the job. It is not known whether Chief Vollmer was really convinced that Wilson was ready for his own command, or if the chief was reacting to the very real possibility that law enforcement would lose the young man forever if immediate action was not taken. In any event, Vollmer strongly suggested to O. W. that he compete for the Fullerton job. After a brief period of indecision, Wilson applied for the position, and with August Vollmer's strong backing received the appointment. Vernis and Orlando began making plans for a move to southern California.

4

FULLERTON AND FAILURE

O. W. was anxious to leave Berkeley and begin his new job. He had not the slightest doubt about his ability to excel in it, or that he would be accepted by his new community. Wilson had seen August Vollmer administer the Berkeley Police Department, and he left confident in the knowledge that this blueprint would furnish him with the guidelines necessary to succeed in Fullerton. Unfortunately for O. W. Wilson, he was not Vollmer, and Fullerton was not Berkeley.

Vernis Haddon Wilson was ecstatic over the prospect of their move to Fullerton: Vernis's mother, to whom she was very close, lived in Los Angeles, only a short distance away; the social activities in southern California were almost limitless; and she would be able to pursue a secret personal ambition. Vernis had played a number of roles in the University's little theatre group, so she hoped some day to embark on a career in motion pictures.[1]

Fullerton was rapidly evolving from an agricultural to a suburban community. Located in Orange County, southeast of Los Angeles, the city had grown from 4,400 citizens to more than 10,000 during the previous decade. Fullerton was governed by an elected five-man board of trustees and a mayor, who served as president of the board. The police department consisted of a chief and seven men, two of whom were motorcycle officers. In 1925, the total departmental budget was $27,500. Administrative responsibility for police operations was vested in the chief; however, a standing committee of five citizens had been appointed by the trustees to oversee the police department. This police committee had authority to supervise the police force and make recommendations to the trustees in matters of operations and personnel administration. Although the community was becoming more and more cosmopolitan, the politics was of the small town genre, the dominant philosophy was conservative, and many older residents had a healthy suspicion of outsiders.

O. W. Wilson's predecessor, Arthur Eells, had been fired. The manner of his dismissal was indicative of the politics which pervaded the town and its police department. Eells had served as chief of police for approximately three years. His accomplishments in office were summarized by the departmental historian, who wrote: "Arthur L. Eells was appointed chief in 1922. History reveals very little happened during the three year term of Eells."[2] Because of Fullerton's rapid growth and an accelerating crime rate, the board of trustees directed its police committee to investigate the department and make recommendations for improving its operations. The study was initiated because, according to the board, "a lack of public confidence in the efficiency of the police department has brought about the necessity of its thorough investigation." When completed, the study was highly critical of Chief Eells and his personnel, especially desk sergeant D. L. Ellis, for whom the committee recommended dismissal. Chief Eells was told by the committee to fire Sergeant Ellis, but he asked it to furnish grounds. When it refused, he declined to take any action. Members of the committee then met secretly with the board of trustees, and at the board meeting of 13 February 1925 Chief Eells was asked by the mayor to submit his resignation immediately. He refused, and by a four-to-one vote Eells was immediately discharged "for the good of the service."[3]

When Wilson went to Fullerton, he was prepared to implement the system of policing which he had learned in Berkeley. He did not reckon on the nature of politics in local government, nor is there any evidence to indicate that he was even slightly concerned with the influence of politics on police operations. In Berkeley, August Vollmer had spent his first years in office learning the realities of municipal politics, and extricating his department from them. Consequently, by the time O. W. Wilson joined the force, Vollmer had been able to insulate his patrolmen from the city's politicians. Since Wilson was never bothered by politics in Berkeley, he assumed that the situation elsewhere was similar. He was to discover the hard way that municipal chiefs of police are often subject to the whims and caprices of elected public officials. Chief's learned to either operate in that environment or devote a great deal of time and effort to insulating themselves from it, as Vollmer had done. Wilson's political naïvete and his youthful impatience put him on a collision course with his new superiors.

O. W. Wilson was formally appointed chief of police in Fullerton on the first of April 1925 at a monthly salary of $250. The pay was considerably greater than he had been making in Berkeley, so Vernis and he moved into what to them was a plush suite in Fullerton's California Hotel. It had a kitchen, a formal dining room, a parlor, and a separate bedroom. The Wilson's new home was in the center of town, close to police headquarters.

O. W. immediately plunged into his job, cheerfully working twelve-hour days. Fullerton's officers had been given little direction prior to Wilson: scientific crime detection methods were unknown, the work routine was slovenly, no crime reporting system had been installed, and there was no way headquarters could communicate with patrolmen in the field. O. W. brought his Berkeley training to bear in Fullerton, but one of his most effective weapons was Vernis. She was, according to her best friend, "a social whiz." She entertained often, attended teas, social gatherings, and women's clubs frequently, and generally fulfilled a strong supporting role for her husband, who needed all the aid he could muster.

Chief Wilson had a brief tenure in Fullerton. Yet in his few months of service, he accomplished a great deal. One of his first major innovations was to introduce a crime reporting system into the police department. In the absence of surplus money in the budget to print new forms, he had August Vollmer send him a shipment of Berkeley police reports. O. W. modified the forms so that officers could check off a listing of items, rather than spend long hours writing narrative reports. This would be typical of his efforts in later years, where he would adopt a Vollmer idea, then revise it to suit his purposes.

Wilson persuaded city fathers to install a Gamewell light system in order to reduce the time it took for officers to respond to calls. Red lights were located atop the city's three tallest buildings, where field officers, regardless of their locations, could see them and call headquarters for messages.[4]

Fullerton owned two police cars. Wilson conducted a study which determined that it would be more feasible for the city to dispose of these cars and pay officers a monthly vehicle allowance of $45 to use their own cars. Thus, the city would have the use of eight cars, instead of two, they would not be faced with maintenance problems, and the men would be more inclined to take better care of their equipment. The board of trustees, impressed with the logic of Wilson's recommendation, adopted it.[5]

The innovations instituted by Chief Wilson were aimed at upgrading the department's service to the community. New report forms, Gamewell lights, privately owned police cars, all were designed to improve Fullerton's crime fighting efficiency, which had been called into serious question under Chief Eells. Wilson did not have immediate access to a local university, or to a police training school, so he conducted in-service training sessions himself. He was in the process of holding weekly seminars on scientific crime investigation, when he was afforded an opportunity to offer his men and the community a firsthand demonstration. A local teenager had been arrested and accused by the police of burglarizing a local garage. He denied the allegation. Chief Wilson examined the crime scene and discovered several footprints in the ground just under the forced entry. The chief made a plaster cast of the imprint, compared it to the boy's shoe, and obtained a confession from his suspect when it matched. The local newspaper reported the incident with considerable enthusiasm:

> There was no longer any doubt of the prisoner's guilt. When confronted by the evidence, Pete made a prompt and thorough confession. Yesterday he entered the county jail for a thirty day stay during which time he may muse on the wonders of scientific police methods.[6]

Chief Wilson's department made another arrest which gave him satisfaction. A suspicious person was stopped by patrolmen for a traffic violation. When they searched their records they found that he was wanted for embezzlement in Berkeley. He was returned there for trial. August Vollmer wrote Wilson a letter of appreciation which must have been gratefully received.[7]

Not all of Chief Wilson's ideas and innovations were warmly accepted. O. W., the inveterate "black letter man," decided to strictly enforce Fullerton's animal control ordinance. He issued a statement to the press that all dogs must be kept on leash. Any animals found roaming the streets, licensed or not, would be impounded and destroyed. Dog owners throughout the community responded in outrage, not at the ordinance, but at their chief's intention to enforce it. Wilson was exposed to his first taste of small town politics when the police committee chastised him for overaggressiveness.[8]

On another occasion, the chief recommended discontinuance of the police department's two-man motorcycle detail. Motorcycles were expensive to operate and maintain, accident prone, of no value in inclement weather, unusable on the midnight shift, and noisy. In effect, they had limitations which made them a serious liability. Throughout his career, O. W. Wilson was to view motorcycles as a liability to law enforcement, and, when he was in a position to do so, would sharply curtail their use. Wilson recommended their abolition to the board of trustees. By a three-to-two vote, the board concurred, but only after a public controversy which alienated the two motorcycle officers and merchants, such as the local undertaker, whose funeral processions had been traditionally furnished escorts by the officers.[9]

Chief Wilson had been taught by August Vollmer that a successful chief of police communicates regularly with the community. Vollmer rarely missed an opportunity to address a civic or professional group. Because of his early association with California's most famous chief, and the early publicity he had received as a protégé of Vollmer, Wilson was in demand as a speaker. He felt that the town was somewhat bucolic, so he set about to expose citizens to some of the ideas he had encountered in social science classes at the University of California. Many of his ideas were not popular.

Chief Wilson had become interested in the causes and prevention of crime. A study of criminality in one family, Richard Dugdale's *The Jukes* had been assigned reading in one of Wilson's classes. The study traced 1,200 persons of Jukes blood and discovered an incredibly high number had been committed to jails and poorhouses. Money expended by the state in supporting, lodging, treating, and incarcerating members of the Jukes family totaled more than one million dollars in seventy-five years. As a consequence, some thought had been given to the sterilization of criminal "types." Although there is no evidence to indicate that Wilson himself believed in sterilization, he did feel an obligation to discuss the idea. Unfortunately, the forum in which he brought it up was a church social group. O. W. had been accustomed to a university environment in which even the most controversial ideas could be aired. Fullerton's citizens, however, did not appear to be ready for such dialogue, as Wilson discovered well before the furor over his speech calmed down.

O. W. had also been exposed to the "concentric circle" theory of crime, in which the greatest concentration of crime in cities was in the most heavily populated areas, and decreased as the population lessened. Thus, to Wilson there was a clearcut correlation between population and crime. While addressing a local civic group, he explained that one cause of crime, in his judgment, was population density. He submitted a possible solution: population control. When asked for specificity by a member of the audience, he explained that some form of birth control was in order. The speech caused a sensation.[10]

Chief Wilson had performed well in his new job; but, members of the police committee soon became convinced that despite his good work, O. W. was simply not worth the complaints he was generating from prominent citizens. He had made many friends in the community, so the committee was not enthusiastic about recommending his dismissal. Instead, a committee member approached the chief in private and asked him to resign because of a lack of administrative experience, and because his plans for reorganization were too ambitious for a small department. He could have stayed and fought dismissal, but that was not his style. O. W.

submitted, without comment, his resignation to the board of trustees, effective 1 December 1925. He steadfastly refused to publicly discuss his decision or to openly criticize public officials or citizens.[11] On the day he resigned, Wilson and Vernis left Fullerton.

O. W. Wilson moved to Los Angeles, secure in the knowledge that he had done the best job in Fullerton of which he was capable. He never once doubted his ability as a chief of police. Embittered as he was over this crushing experience, he felt that Fullerton simply was not ready for reform. He also decided that he had no place in law enforcement, for he would not compromise his principles in order to hold any job. The police service was in need of reform, but if reform ever came it would do so without O. W. Wilson. He then committed himself to a career in business.[12]

O. W. and Vernis moved into a modest Los Angeles apartment. The only piece of furniture was a piano. Wilson applied for and landed an investigative position with Pacific Finance Corporation, where his primary duties were to conduct background investigations on credit applicants and repossess automobiles. At first, the work was interesting. The pay was significantly less than O. W. had made in Fullerton, but there was more time for an active social life, and the Wilsons immersed themselves in it.

The nagging feeling of regret that O. W. had over his Fullerton experience was initially blunted by Vernis's insistence that they fill almost every free moment with activity. During the days they usually went swimming or surfing. Nights meant a bridge game, dinner with friends, long rides, or lengthy conversations in the Wilson apartment, which was slowly being furnished one piece at a time. Weekends often meant short trips: to San Diego to visit the Wilson family, to the hills north of Los Angeles to hike, to Berkeley for sporting events.[13] Meanwhile, Mrs. Wilson embarked on her motion picture career.

Shortly after arriving in Los Angeles, Vernis registered with the Motion Picture Casting Service, a placement agency for actors, actresses, and stunt men and women. She never questioned her destiny to achieve stardom in the movie industry, though work was not immediately forthcoming. After a time, however, Vernis began to receive bit parts. Because of her swimming and diving experience, she was soon in demand for stunt work. In one scene Vernis, standing in for the star, dived into the sea from a moving ocean liner and swam to her lover on the beach. Her roles became progressively more important.

O. W.'s career with Pacific Finance was not going well. He received little satisfaction from the work, which Wilson began regarding as undignified. The remuneration was not sufficient to offset the drabness of the duties, and his path toward promotion appeared blocked by senior men. He was on the brink of applying for a patrolman's position with the Los Angeles Police Department when in the spring of 1928 August Vollmer approached him about returning to law enforcement as a chief.

A major scandal in the city of Wichita had resulted in the dismissal of the police chief. The city manager was determined to find a scrupulously honest chief who would completely reorganize the police department, so he contacted Vollmer for a recommendation. Without hesitation, Chief Vollmer referred the manager to O. W. Wilson. An exchange of letters between the city manager and Wilson resulted in an offer to interview for the job. It was met with indecision on O. W.'s part. He had heard that Wichita was a church-going town, replete with blue laws. Consequently, he had misgivings about being accepted by citizens. He confided in August Vollmer that:

> I hate to go through life being a hypocrite. Yet since leaving Fullerton I haven't been to church over half a dozen times, I smoke cigarettes and so does my wife, we play bridge at a tenth or twentieth, and have even enjoyed intoxicating liquor. And I don't feel even mildly wicked or immoral. What would the population of Wichita or any other town think of that? [14]

Wilson's concern over possible intolerance in Wichita was compounded by the fact that its city manager was a Quaker. He was reassured by Vollmer that the community was not so puritanical that it would condemn him for his moderate indulgences. In March of 1928, after a great deal of thought, he notified the city manager of Wichita that he was interested in the job. [15]

Vernis Wilson was less than enthusiastic over a possible move to Wichita, for she felt strongly that she was on the brink of stardom. Vernis would reluctantly accompany her husband to Kansas, convinced that she had left fame and fortune behind. The lingering bitterness over this decision was to contribute to a general deterioration in the Wilson's marital relationship. But O. W. Wilson had made a decision to which he was unalterably committed.

5

THE WEST POINT OF LAW
ENFORCEMENT:
WILSON IN WICHITA

The Wichita in which O. W. Wilson would settle was not considerably different from the one Wyatt Earp had policed fewer than fifty years before. The population had increased to more than 100,000 residents, and the "cow town" image had slowly passed into history.[1] Nevertheless, the Wichita Police Department had failed to keep pace with the demands of an increasingly cosmopolitan community. Wyatt Earp was gone, but his legacy of heavy-handed law enforcement and venal corruption appeared to be the dominant features of the Wichita Police Department.

Prior to 1928, Wichita policemen were hired on the recommendation of another police officer, an influential businessman, or a politician. There were no entry level standards, no training, no promotional policies, and no code of conduct. Officers were simply hired, sworn in, issued police equipment, assigned a beat, and told to police the city. As a consequence, violent crime was rampant, graft flourished, incompetence was the rule, and brutality was commonplace.

The propensity of Wichita policemen to use excessive physical force in making arrests earned for the police department a reputation for cruelty. In one instance, the proprietor of a fruit stand was battered into unconsciousness by two officers who had arrested him for possessing a bottle of illegal liquor. The bottle was later found to contain soda. In another incident, a local juvenile was badly beaten by the head of the department's vice squad. The youth, who had been arrested for fighting, was later acquitted in court. A traveling salesman was falsely arrested in his hotel room for possession of alcohol by officers who had illegally entered and searched the room. Since the salesman did not drink, some citizens assumed that the arresting officers had made a mistake, which they tried to correct by framing their suspect.[2] These "sledgehammer tactics" became a major issue when *Harper's* devoted an article to the Wichita police and other departments which used this approach.[3]

Although the police attacked law-abiding citizens and petty criminals with depressing regularity, they showed much less enthusiasm for contacts with major criminals, or for suppressing organized vice activities, especially bootlegging. When community leaders demanded an end to police inaction in the face of rampant vice, Chief Ike Walston responded by disbanding his vice squad, declaring a "war on punchboards,"[4] and taking the handcuffs from his men. The Independent Grocers' Association officially censured the police department over the dramatic increase of armed robberies, and the absence of arrests. The grocers demanded "better policemen, and more of them" and warned city officials that "if the police won't protect us, we will defend ourselves."[5]

On 10 June 1927 a group of thirty-seven prominent attorneys formed the Association for Protection of Civil Rights. The association pledged to end police abuses by filing damage suits against lawless policemen, by seeking indictments against officers who had flagrantly violated civil liberties, and by acting as a watchdog over police excesses. The situation crystallized when a state attorney general's investigation revealed that many Wichita policemen, including high ranking officers, were on the payroll of bootleggers. Chief Walston was dismissed, and City Manager Bert Wells set out to find a successor.[6]

Almost immediately, Wichita's political officials and special interest groups began to exert pressure on Wells to appoint a local man to the vacant chief's position. Wells resisted. He believed that the malaise which gripped the police department would continue under a local chief. As a result, he did what many other public administrators had done in similar circumstances: he contacted August Vollmer. Vollmer's recommendation of O. W. Wilson led Wells to extend an invitation to Wilson to come to Wichita for an interview.

O. W. came to Wichita amidst rumors that the city's American Legion Post had convinced the city manager that he should hire a Wichita resident who was a veteran of World War I.[7] In fact, the influence exerted on Bert Wells to do just that was intense. Wells, however, was a man who, though politically astute, exercised independent judgment in such matters. The manager was a quiet man who had previously been city engineer. His penchant for formal dress and stiff collars made him appear sterner than he was. Wells was committed to honesty and efficiency in government, and although he in no way considered himself a liberal, he did pride himself on being a "good government" man whose commitment to integrity in government was rivaled only by his interest in fiscal responsibility.[8] Wells interviewed several potential chiefs of police, but he was especially impressed by Wilson, despite O. W.'s youth and lack of experience. The city manager later remarked that of all the candidates, Wilson was the only one "able to look me square in the eye." City Manager Wells had already decided to hire O. W. before he introduced him to a group of business and professional men, who were also favorably impressed by Wilson.[9]

On 27 March 1928, Bert Wells announced that he had selected O. W. Wilson as Wichita's next chief of police at a monthly salary of $335. Wilson accepted the appointment. Thus began one of the most productive tenures in the history of American police administration.

O. W. Wilson's eleven-year term of service in Wichita has been evaluated by only one historian, who overlooked a number of important Wilsonian contributions to law enforcement while alleging that he was merely emulating August Vollmer's programs in Berkeley. Jane Robinson Howard, August Vollmer's biographer, was so impressed with Vollmer's apparent impact on Wilson's Wichita career that she titled a chapter "Training by Correspondence: Vollmer's Influence on Orlando Wilson, Berkeley's Most Famous College Cop."[10] What Howard was referring to was the seventy letters Vollmer wrote to O. W., informing him how to organize and administer the department, counseling him on community relations and the political realities of law enforcement, advising him how to deal with the myriad problems he would encounter. Indeed, the amount of material Vollmer forwarded to Wilson was massive. Yet, what Howard has failed to sense is that O. W. Wilson discounted much of the information, modified a great deal of it to fit his purposes, and refined Vollmer's rough ideas to a hitherto unknown level. Furthermore, the correspondence between the men was a two-way street, for Wilson answered as many questions as he asked, and Vollmer benefited from Wilson's programs, ideas, and innovations. August Vollmer was a great source of counsel to Wilson, especially during the early years; but O. W. was very much his own man in Wichita. By the time Wilson left Kansas there was no doubt that he had blossomed into a leading force in American police administration.

Wilson telephoned Vernis to tell her that he had accepted the Wichita job, and that he intended to commence work immediately. She agreed to join him after placing their affairs in order in Los Angeles.

It was made abundantly clear to the patrolmen who were on duty on Wilson's first official workday that the Wichita Police Department was in for a drastic change of direction. He called an assembly of officers, at which he promised eventual organizational changes, but not until the present regimen had been thoroughly analyzed. His low-key, almost scholarly presentation, was a marked contrast to the bluff, coarse demeanor of his predecessor. During an initial tour of headquarters, Chief Wilson saw a deck of playing cards in the squad room. "Get rid of those playing cards," he quietly ordered, thereby eliminating the daily game which had become a squad room tradition. When he inspected the department's lockup, Wilson could not help but notice that the booking room door was painted red. His request for an explanation was met by evasiveness. To Wilson, the red door and the silence it caused among his officers meant that the garish color was designed to hide blood stains. He left headquarters only after giving instructions to have the door painted white by the following morning.[11]

In a letter to Wilson, August Vollmer cautioned the young chief to move slowly in his reform efforts and only after careful consultation with his superiors.[12] O. W. thanked Vollmer for his advice, then studiously ignored. it. His first year in office was a whirlwind of activity. Chief Wilson set about to cleanse his department of corruption by weeding out and dismissing officers whom he even suspected of misconduct. Throwing caution to the winds, he fired six officers, including one captain, and forced the resignation of fifteen others. Thus, over 20 percent of the hundred-man police department left the service in 1928.[13]

To impress on his officers the necessity of mastering their jobs, he initiated weekly quizzes in the squadroom, a procedure which "made the boys at police headquarters frankly nervous." He tested the officers' ability to recall facts by furnishing lists of numbers which they were asked to repeat later, administered psychological tests designed to measure aggressive tendencies, asked officers to secretly rate their colleagues, and made all patrolmen take an I. Q. test, much to the consternation of veterans, one of whom complained, "How do I know how many wives Henry VIII had and how is that going to show whether I can clean up a burglary job."[14]

Wilson began an active in-service training program. Although space in police headquarters was at a premium, he established a small library and converted a spare room to a gymnasium. Daily instruction was given in jujitsu. On his training program, Wilson stated that:

> Considerable attention has been given to the personnel; every effort being made to strengthen them physically, mentally, and morally, and to build up within their ranks a spirit of loyalty, service, and pride in department and self.[15]

Upon entering office, Chief Wilson found that only thirty-five of his hundred officers were assigned to automobile patrol duty. He initiated an immediate departmental reorganization designed to increase by one-third the patrol force. He eliminated unnecessary foot patrolmen, discontinued the use of some motorcycle units, and reassigned clerical and administrative personnel to motorized patrol.[16] In addition, Wilson recreated the vice squad, placed his three most trusted officers in it, and instructed them to strictly enforce all vice laws, especially bootlegging, prostitution and gambling. He painstakingly pointed out, however, that the enforcement of all laws must be carried out in an even-handed manner, consistent with constitutional and statutory restraints.[17]

Wilson next turned his attention to establishing a records and police report system. He drafted report forms for all types of police cases, issued work sheets to all officers whereby they were made accountable for their on-duty time, and created an M. O. file to assist in the detection of burglars and robbers who had fallen into a criminal pattern. A rather simple scheme of filing the reports in coded case jackets allowed quick retrieval of reports. When August Vollmer was apprised of the new record scheme, he praised Wilson for creating a system which was "the first of its kind."[18]

Since the establishment of a comprehensive records scheme was only an aid in criminal investigations, Chief Wilson began studying ways to improve the department's followup investigative capability. In his mind, he separated detectives and potential detectives into two distinct classes: producers and nonproducers. With cold precision, he fired, demoted, disciplined, transferred, or forced resignations from officers he had identified as deadwood. Productive officers were rewarded by promotions and reassignment to the detective division. Once the nonproducers had been swept aside and replaced by Wilson's handpicked men, the chief subdivided detectives into the following functional specialties: armed robbery, larceny, burglary, pawnshops, auto theft, and vice.[19] Wilson expected his detectives to develop an expertise in their assigned area, and he personally offered instruction to them, while stocking the newly formed departmental library with the latest criminology texts. When O. W. found that several of the leading books on crime were in German and French, he had them translated at a local university.[20]

After several months of observing his patrol officers in action, he became convinced that they would be unable to provide the type of service that the community needed until some form of communications could be installed which allowed police headquarters to communicate with the radioless patrol cars. Wilson petitioned the city manager for funds to install a Gamewell light network. A cooperative Bert Wells persuaded his city council to appropriate the needed money, and the twenty call boxes and forty-two warning lights which were installed represented a more comprehensive system than the one in Berkeley.[21]

Two of his first year innovations met with general disapproval from the rank and file. The officers' discontent slowed Wilson's reform efforts not one whit. Amidst the shrill criticism of veteran officers, the chief passed an order which called for the photographing and finger-printing of all policemen "for record purposes." Officers who didn't approve of the new order were invited to resign. All fingerprints and photographs were filed with the United States Department of Justice, much to the consternation of the men, who generally felt that it placed them in the same category as criminals.[22]

Of all his new ideas, one raised an intense storm of protest in the ranks of patrolmen: the exclusive use of one-man patrol cars in the field, even during night shifts. Throughout his career, Wilson was to become an outspoken champion of this plan. Criticism of it never died down, es-pecially from patrolmen. Wilson pointed out to officers and city officials that to redeploy men in one-man cars would provide twice the number of patrol units, at only minimal extra cost. The chief indicated that a man riding alone at night was more likely to be cautious than if he had a partner, and therefore less apt to be carelessly injured while on routine patrol. Moreover, Chief Wilson felt that when officers worked in tandem they were more inclined to loaf and socialize. The patrolmen's pleas for their chief to reconsider his radical new concept fell on deaf ears.

In order to win public confidence in his beleaguered agency, O. W. cast about for a concept which would impress on the community the new philosophy of service he was attempting to instill in the Wichita Police Department. He decided to label his agency "The Square Deal Depart-ment." It was a way of informing citizens and police officers alike that the community was entitled to receive "a square deal" from policemen. Consistent with this promise, Wilson drafted and publicized a "Square Deal Code" that pledged his personnel to high moral and ethical behavior, promised professional service to the public, committed officers to obey the law and to practice restraint in the face of provocation, and affirmed a desire to remain scrupulously honest despite temptations to do other-wise. Wilson termed it a "Ten Commandments" for law enforcement. It is doubtful if even he realized at the time the historical significance of this Square Deal Code, which thus far has been overlooked by police historians. Wilson's code was the forerunner of a Law Enforcement Code of Ethics which was adopted by the International Association of Chiefs of Police (IACP) at their 1957 convention. Police historians have traced the origins of this code to a 1952 meeting of California police chiefs and professors at which a code of ethics for state policemen was articulated.

The California Code was adopted virtually intact, by the IACP. O. W. Wilson, then Dean of the School of Criminology at the University of California at Berkeley, was at the meeting, and a member of the committee appointed to the subcommittee charged with articulating the code, along with two of his professors. A comparison between the Square Deal Code of 1928 and the "Law Enforcement Code of Ethics" of 1952 clearly indicates that the former code formed the basis of the latter. (Both are reprinted in the Appendix.) Thus, O. W. Wilson was the father of a police code of ethics which has gained universal acceptance in the field, although he was never given credit for it.[23]

Consistent with his commitment to upgrade the police department, Chief Wilson initiated a program to recruit the best possible men for the growing number of vacancies on the department. He began to administer the Army Alpha Test, forced applicants to submit to psychological evaluations, conducted exhaustive background investigations, and held personal interviews with each prospective officer. Wilson also initiated three weeks of formal recruit training. Lecturers from local educational institutions constituted a major part of the faculty, along with Wilson and his staff.[24]

To promote his new programs, O. W. spoke to Wichita's civic, professional, social, and church groups, and encouraged his officers to do the same. As a consequence, he won widespread support for his reform efforts. Wilson's labors were dramatically rewarded when the League for Protection of Civil Liberties, the consortium of attorneys formed during his predecessor's administration, voted unanimously to disband because, according to its founder, "there is no work for us to do."[25]

A year passed and Chief O. W. Wilson was still in office. He had won over many friends in the community, but he also began making powerful enemies. His rather strict personnel policies meant that the city's politicians no longer had an impact on hiring and promotions. Furthermore, the consistency with which he rooted out and terminated unsatisfactory policemen meant that there was a growing body of former officers in the community to undermine Wilson's reform efforts. Chief Wilson represented a threat to those who felt comfortable with the more traditional ways of policing. Citizens who had previously been extended special privileges by the police department, and who returned the favor in very tangible ways, had no use for Wilson. Chief Wilson made it plain that officers were neither to grant nor receive favors. He set an example when he went to the Spines Clothing Company to purchase a new suit. The proprietor was Jack Spines, a politically powerful local businessman. Wilson quickly found a suit which pleased him, whereupon Spines proudly made him a gift of it. The chief, in rather direct language, informed the shocked haberdasher that it was contrary to departmental policy to accept anything of value, and Spines was never again to corrupt Wichita's officers with such an offer. Wilson paid for the garment and left carrying with him a new suit and the lasting enmity of an influential merchant.

O. W. Wilson had survived his first year in office. His successes were impressive. Thus far, the few enemies he had made were greatly outnumbered by the great mass of citizens who viewed their new chief as a welcome change from Ike Walston. Wilson had alienated powerful interests in the community; nevertheless, he survived, and the police department prospered—thanks in large measure to City Manager Bert Wells, who recognized in his chief a man of superior ability and steadfastly supported and insulated him from the influence of partisan politics.[26] Wilson entered his second year buoyed by his successes, deeply committed to even more radical reform.

O. W. Wilson was convinced that the police service would not be a worthwhile career for a gentleman until its status had been uplifted from that of a mere job to a profession. Although he had no illusions that this evolution would take place overnight, Wilson believed that the objective was attainable. Very early in his Wichita tenure, Chief Wilson dedicated himself to a bold program of reorganization which would not only professionalize his municipal police force, but which would prove to both citizens and public officials across the nation that a police profession was necessary and feasible. He confided in August Vollmer that he would not be satisfied until the Wichita Police Department was the country's finest. O. W. Wilson's reform efforts were designed to produce a model police agency equipped to serve two communities: Wichita, and the broad field of law enforcement. In essence, O. W. felt that he had an obligation to serve the citizens of Wichita; but he sensed that his primary duty was to the police service.[27] Wilson's ability to survive for more than a decade in Wichita was due in large measure to the compatibility of these dual loyalties, and to general public and political approval for his programs. When the two did periodically come into conflict, O. W. inevitably displayed a higher loyalty to his chosen field, and he acted accordingly.

The stock market collapse of 1929 and the resultant depression furnished Chief Wilson with a unique opportunity to attract high quality police recruits who would not otherwise have entered the law enforcement service. For a monthly salary of $150, men who would ordinarily have disdained such duties rushed to apply for positions as police patrolmen. Confronted with this new source of manpower, O. W. quickly upgraded his selection standards to skim off the cream of the crop. He also took extraordinary steps to ensure that his best people remained in law enforcement after the effects of the Depression eased. The chief was not particularly concerned whether or not they stayed with the Wichita Police Department, as long as he could convince them to remain in the police field. In much the same way that August Vollmer had acted as his advocate in the search for a police executive position, so too did Wilson seek to place Wichita officers with leadership capabilities in high level administrative posts nationwide.

The face of the Wichita Police Department changed abruptly under O. W. Wilson. Policies, procedure, philosophy, programs, and organizational structure were reformed, but of all the changes instituted in Wichita none was more striking than the ones concerning personnel. Wilson took extra care in selecting new officers, as witnessed by an article in which he wrote: "As with a wife, selection is much more important than training."[28] In addition to carefully choosing policemen, the chief placed them on probation for one year following appointment. The turnover rate remained high as Chief Wilson continually pruned men he deemed undesirable from the department's ranks. Annual police department reports for the period of 1930 through 1932 indicate that he "dismissed for cause" thirty-three officers, and that seven other officers resigned with charges pending against them. As men, for one reason or another, left the department, they were replaced by younger, more intelligent, and better educated personnel. During his first five years in office, the average entry level test score on the Army Alpha Test went from 79.73 to 108.35, the average age decreased from 39.86 to 36.87, and the mean educational level of officers increased from 9.14 years to 10.42 years. The latter statistic takes on greater significance when one considers that many veteran officers who stayed with the police department were not educated beyond the fifth grade.[29]

As recruitment and selection standards were being raised, Wilson began instituting extraordinary training programs. He started Saturday "crab meetings" at which all off-duty officers were exposed to in-service training. Friends University, a private liberal arts institution in Wichita, provided the services of a professor of municipal administration. The weekly meetings began at noon and usually lasted approximately two hours, following which Wilson conducted a staff conference for supervisors and commanders.[30] Although some of the meetings were devoted to technical and administrative subjects, public and press relations was a favorite Wilson topic. Chief Wilson felt that if his agency was to gain the full acceptance of the community, he had to end the veil of secrecy which had characterized the internal affairs of the police department. He instructed his men to cooperate fully with the press, and to make departmental files open to reporters and the public.[31]

O. W. slowly expanded his recruit training school to six weeks of intensified instruction. In 1930, Wilson supplemented his preservice and in-service training program by ordering his men to report for work one-half hour prior to their tours of duty. During this period, the assembled officers would be lectured on various aspects of police work. The procedure was instituted as a regular part of the training regimen. "Roll-call training" was later to become an accepted practice of municipal law enforcement agencies, which found that, because of scheduling problems, it often represented the only way in which continuing in-service training could be carried out. A police historian has traced the origins of roll-call training back to 1948, when "the Los Angeles Police Department inaugurated the first roll call continuation training program in the country."[32] Obviously, it was O. W. Wilson who pioneered the concept, as the Wichita plan predated roll-call training in Los Angeles by some eighteen years.

In 1931, O. W. Wilson became the focus of attention of two warring Wichita newspapers. The *Beacon* and the *Eagle* had always been friendly rivals; but, when the *Beacon* was purchased in 1928 by Max, John, and Louis Levand, the natural rivalry between the two papers was transformed into a vendetta. The Levand brothers had served for many years with the *Denver Post,* which was owned by Frederick G. Bonfils. By specializing in sensationalism, the *Post* had been able to dramatically increase its circulation, until it had become one of the most widely read newspapers in the West. Striking out on their own, the Levands decided to invest in the *Beacon* and institute the methods of yellow journalism which they had learned from Bonfils. The *Eagle,* on the other hand, was a home-owned newspaper. Its publishers were Victor and Marcellus Murdock, and although the *Eagle* was not above sensationalizing certain stories, it had earned a reputation for responsible journalism.[33] Both newspapers supported O. W. Wilson during his first years in office. As the *Eagle* emerged as a champion of Chief Wilson, however, the *Beacon*'s staff almost instinctively became less enthusiastic about him.[34] In 1931, an incident occurred which allowed the *Beacon* to finally abandon its support of Wilson.

Wilbur Underhill was a notorious midwestern bank robber and killer. He escaped from the Oklahoma Penitentiary in 1931 and fled to Wichita, where he decided to stay until it was safe to surface. Underhill hid in a rooming house on South Water Street. Acting on information received from an anonymous citizen, Merle Colver, a popular Wichita patrolman, went to the hotel. When he attempted to arrest Underhill, the escapee shot and killed him. A massive manhunt resulted in Underhill's capture by a former Wichita policeman who had been dismissed by Chief Wilson for drinking on duty. The *Eagle* factually covered the story, but the

Beacon chose to attack Wilson for culpability in his officer's murder.[35]

The *Beacon* blamed Merle Colver's death on Wilson's one-man patrol policy. It accused the chief of risking his officers' lives because of economic considerations and administrative convenience. The *Beacon* did not report that during the previous eleven years, nine men had been killed in the line of duty, all but one of whom were patrolling with partners. A further controversy developed when prominent members of the community, at the *Beacon*'s urging, pressed O. W. to rehire the former Wichita officer who had captured Wilbur Underhill.[36] Wilson remained steadfast on both points. He refused the abandon the one-man car principle. Although the chief never stated so publicly, Colver had violated departmental policy by failing to wait for another officer before attempting to arrest Underhill. The idea was sound, so the Chief would not capitulate simply to avoid bad publicity. On the matter of reinstating the former officer he would not rescind his original action. To O. W. the issue had not been the officer's courage, but his lack of ethics. City Manager Bert Wells supported his chief, who weathered the storm, though the *Beacon* had unalterably turned against him.[37]

O. W. Wilson had almost completely submerged himself in work. Laboring into the evening, often seven days a week, his social life consisted almost exclusively of speeches before community groups. Because of his anticorruption stance, Wilson thought it essential that he back up his demands for individual honesty with unannounced inspections of headquarters and patrol zones during the late evening and early morning hours. It became commonplace for officers to encounter their chief at the scene of calls on an afternoon or midnight shift. He confided to no one where he would be at any given time. His men began to conduct themselves as though Wilson was inevitably enroute to their locations, which was exactly the purpose of these inspections. To O. W. Wilson, a police officer's conduct in the community was to be above reproach at all times.[38] This commitment to excellence was to become a Wilson trademark. Nonetheless, Wilson was paying a price for his dedication.

He continued making powerful enemies. When, for example, Jack Priest, an influential businessman, asked Chief Wilson to fix a speeding ticket, Wilson in quite explicit terms told Priest that the citation could expeditiously be fixed by taking it to the court clerk and paying the appropriate fine. Wilson took special care to indicate to his police officers that the era of extending special privileges to selected citizens was over. There was a restaurant in Wichita named the Ringside, in which high stakes gambling had been allowed to flourish, unhindered by the police, at least prior to Chief Wilson's tenure. The restaurant was owned by Max Cohen, a former associate of Chicago gangster, Al Capone. It was common knowledge that Cohen used the second floor of his restaurant to accommodate those citizens who wished to engage in a game of chance. O. W., learning of the situation, planted an undercover policeman on the premises to gather evidence. A subsequent raid netted Cohen and seventeen of his customers. Wilson watched as each of the gamblers was loaded into the awaiting paddy wagon. The policeman escorting Max Cohen, however, placed him in a patrol car. O. W., seeing this, brusquely advised the officer to "put him in the wagon with everyone else." The police officer was later counseled about the evils of granting special considerations to a privileged few.[39]

The demands O. W. constantly made on himself deprived the Wilsons of a normal home life. Vernis had never been enthusiastic about their move to Wichita. Now, with her husband gone both day and night, she was increasingly alone. Any hope for an active social life had been all but eliminated. In 1931, O. W. and Vernis had a son, Henry Haddon Wilson. It was a bright spot in a marriage which was slowly moving toward dissolution.

If the Depression was furnishing O. W. Wilson with a wealth of fresh manpower, it was costing him in other ways. The nation's economic collapse had made it necessary for local government to economize. The tax base of cities had been drastically reduced, and the ability of citizens to financially support new municipal projects was limited. Responding to this need to economize, public officials moved to implement governmental austerity programs. Wichita was no exception to this general condition, and the police department was not overlooked in the municipal belt tightening process. Wilson argued strenuously for budget increases to fund his innovations. City Manager Wells supported his chief's budget requests whenever he could, but Wells was forced to manage a city administration which consisted of department heads whose expectations far outweighed his ability to fulfill them.[40] One of the projects with which Chief Wilson encountered funding problems was a one-way radio system. He wished to have radios installed in his vehicles with receiving but not sending capabilities. Later, as communication technology improved and additional fiscal resources became available, he planned to have two-way radios installed. Although Bert Wells was sympathetic to the plan, he simply did not have the money to support it. Chief Wilson, convinced that the addition of this new communication equipment would greatly increase his ability to fight crime, moved to overcome the city's opposition. He asked his men to take a monthly pay cut of five dollars. Wilson had his annual salary reduced from $4,800 to $3,956, and relinquished his right to the use of a city vehicle. O. W.'s salary was never restored to its original amount, nor was he ever issued a city car. But that year the police vehicles were equipped with one-way radios, and before he left Wichita two-way radios were in use.[41]

Chief Wilson had become convinced that no single municipal police department could provide for itself the training necessary to adequately upgrade personnel. Only major departments located in urban areas usually had the resources to provide for expert instruction in the wide range of subjects which made up police work. Professional law enforcement was in its fledgling stage, so that there were relatively few police experts available in the field. Those who were available were either concentrated in a number of metropolitan areas, such as New York, Chicago, Philadelphia, Washington, and Detroit, or in academic communities, such as Berkeley, Evanston, Ann Arbor, and Cambridge. Moreover, few municipal police chiefs could afford to bring these experts, individually or in groups, to their departments for lectures. O. W. Wilson moved to create a structure whereby police chiefs in Kansas could make use of the police experts which were scattered around the country.

He approached the Kansas League of Municipalities and petitioned its governing board to create a police training school. The school would be held annually, the faculty would be made up of people of preeminence in their individual fields, and the students would come from police agencies across the state. The League of Municipalities decided to sponsor Wilson's idea. He was made director of the school. The first course of instruction was held in Wichita in 1931. During the next ten years, the school was expanded in size. It was O. W. Wilson's responsibility to construct each program and assemble the faculty. He used the opportunity to invite to Wichita some of the most distinguished men in and on the periphery of law enforcement. In so doing, Chief Wilson brought to Kansas a wealth of expertise which would have otherwise been unavailable to the state's policemen. Professionally, he profited from it more than his colleagues. While the school's faculty members were in Wichita, he brought them into the department to teach and to make recommendations for improvement. The chief also had Wichita officers attend the training school and pass on the information they learned to other Wichita officers. At one training school, forty-five of the eighty-two officers in attendance were from Wichita.[42] Wilson also profited personally from the school. Many of the distinguished lecturers were surprised and pleased to learn that there was a model police department evolving in the heart of the midwest. When they returned home, the tale of O. W. Wilson and his Wichita Police Department was spread. Many of his lecturers came from the federal government: the FBI, the Secret Service, the Treasury Department, the Bureau of Narcotics, and the Prohibition Bureau. Others came from major police agencies, such as the New York and Chicago Police departments. Still others traveled from universities, such as Harvard and Northwestern. Among his most distinguished lecturers were Dr. Karl Menninger; Franklin Kreml, Director of the Traffic Division, International Association of Chiefs of Police; Quinn Tamm, an assistant director of the FBI; Leonarde Keeler, developer of the polygraph; J. Stannard Baker, Director of Research for Northwestern University's Traffic Institute; Fred Inbau, professor of law at Northwestern University; and Donald Stone, Director of the Public Information Service in Chicago.[43] Throughout his public life, Wilson was to encounter these men, several of whom played important roles in his career.

As the men who had been recruited to police work since Wilson's takeover in Wichita gained experience, the chief opened promotional opportunities by either firing veteran commanders or creating new command positions. By the mid-1930's, most of the Wichita Police Department's command staff were Wilson men. C. D. Murrell, Ray Ashworth, William K. (Tex) Ingram, A. A. Lewis, E. P. Moomau, and C. V. Bedell were all elevated to captain with fewer than eight years seniority, an almost unheard-of occurrence in municipal law enforcement. To speed their ascension, Wilson swept older officers aside with disdain. If he could find grounds for discipline, he often summarily dismissed them from the service. If no clearcut grounds, other than personal slovenliness, were apparent, the chief would either reduce them in rank or transfer them. A favorite Wilson tactic was to identify officers whom he viewed as undesirable, then transfer them to the city prison farm. This was his way of informing policemen that it would be wise for them to seek other employment. Many of Wichita's officers believed that this was a heavy-handed way to deal with even the most incompetent men, but Wilson was firmly committed to purging the department of deadwood, and he was not particularly concerned about the manner in which that was carried out. When Leonarde Keeler introduced O. W. to the intricacies of the polygraph, the chief was furnished with another method of ensuring departmental integrity. Officers who were suspected of the slightest infraction, or who shirked their duties, were forced to submit to polygraph examinations. Refusal to submit to a test or failure to successfully pass one meant immediate dismissal.[44]

O. W.'s philosophy of discipline is best illustrated in an incident which Wichita's newspapers termed "the Red-Headed Mary Case." Many of Wichita's officers frequented a small cafe next to police headquarters. Working in the cafe was a lovely, nineteen-year-old waitress named Mary Robinson. Mary, a striking red-head, had moved from rural Kansas to Wichita in search of excitement. She found Wichita's police officers intriguing, with their military uniforms and high powered automobiles.

Mary struck up a friendship with a number of patrolmen, who often escorted her to and from work. Her relationship with some officers went beyond mere friendship and, according to the *Wichita Beacon,* "each day one of them would be the recipient of Mary's treasured favor."[45]

One afternoon, Mary Robinson was involved in a minor traffic accident. The patrolman assigned to conduct the investigation was not acquainted with Mary, and he placed her under arrest for causing the accident. Mary resisted, stating "You can't arrest me, I'm the sweetheart of the force." The officer took Mary into custody. She was brought before Chief O. W. Wilson, who learned of her relationship with nine of his officers. Incensed, he called the officers singly into his office and asked each if they had engaged in sexual relations with Mary. The first eight officers denied the charge, whereupon they were immediately fired for lying.[46] The ninth man admitted his transgression, placing Wilson in a quandary. He had fired the first eight for lying, but this last man had told the truth. Wilson commended the man for his truthfulness, then suspended him for thirty days for using bad judgment. Wichita's newspapers reported the story in sensational headlines; however, the press and the general public were never informed of the existence of the ninth man, who returned to work and eventually rose to a responsible position with the police department.[47]

As Wichita's crime statistics were tabulated by Wilson, he found that in every year since he entered office, the ratio of serious crimes per thousand citizens went down, while each year Wichita's solution rate was considerably higher than the national average. Nevertheless, Chief Wilson never missed an opportunity to reevaluate even his most cherished programs. For example, he conducted a statistical study to determine just how valuable his M. O. file was. The M. O. file, highly developed by Vollmer and now in vogue throughout the country, was generally considered an invaluable tool in identifying and apprehending career criminals.[48] Wilson undertook the study to prove to police chiefs who did not use M. O. files that they were overlooking a device of major importance. Instead, he found the reverse was true. In a survey of crime statistics collected over a nine-year period, O. W. discovered that the reason for using M. O. records was based upon a faulty assumption. The assumption was that when career criminals, especially burglars and robbers, had perfected the skills of their vocation, they did not radically depart from a rather discernible pattern. In his study, however, Wilson found that criminals do not usually fall into predictable habits, with the exception of certain specialists, such as safecrackers. Furthermore, he found that a massive number of crimes were random acts committed by juveniles. Wilson concluded that the collection of M. O. files on all general crimes was largely a waste of time and effort. He recommended that such records only be kept on offenses which were most often committed by professional criminals who had adopted marked techniques which they rarely revised. Thus, Wilson had called into serious question the validity of a device which he had learned from August Vollmer, which he had enthusiastically embraced himself, and which was fast becoming dogma in law enforcement. A spinoff of his study was O. W.'s vital concern with the growing frequency with which juveniles engaged in criminal acts. He moved swiftly to reverse what he considered to be an alarming trend toward juvenile delinquency.

O. W. Wilson created a crime prevention bureau, the objective of which was to stem the tide of juvenile crime. Personnel assigned to the unit were to be concerned more with corrections than enforcement, a radical departure from law enforcement practice. One of the first specialists he employed to engage in crime prevention activities was Pearl L'Heureux, who held a master's degree in social welfare from the University of Colorado. Wilson, in another dramatic movement away from accepted police practice, refused to give Miss L'Heureux the title "policewoman." Instead, she was the "juvenile supervisor," and he fixed her salary equivalent to that of her male counterparts. Later, Miss L'Heureux was appointed captain of police, the first woman in American police history to hold that rank in a municipal agency.

O. W. Wilson charged the new unit with responsibility for "keeping crime from occurring by regulating places where it could originate, be taught or fostered, and by directing young people toward a career that would not lead them to commit illegal acts."[49] Part of the division's responsibility was rather traditional. Officers were assigned to inspect dance halls, poolrooms, and other places normally frequented by juveniles. But the idea of "directing people toward a career that would not lead them to commit illegal acts" was a new role for policemen. Such activities had traditionally been reserved for the courts and correctional workers. However, Wilson knew that the juvenile court in Wichita was grossly understaffed, and that its judge, Clyde M. Hudson, was a highly political individual who was not particularly innovative in his treatment of young people.[50] The chief approached Judge Hudson and outlined a plan for attacking juvenile delinquency. Hudson gave the chief's plan his blessing, and Wilson implemented it, not knowing that the judge would later turn on him.

Wilson knew that the traditional manner in which policemen attacked adult crime would not be effective in combating juvenile delinquency. The police strategy in dealing with major adult crime was to aggressively investigate a crime after it occurred in hope that an early arrest could be made. Wilson felt that this was basically a negative strategy. He designed a program which would identify a potential juvenile delinquent before he committed a major crime so that an attempt could be made to change the course of his life before the youngster committed an illegal act. He had two terms for this plan: "human engineering," and "adjustment work."

Chief Wilson contacted social scientists at both Friends University and the Municipal University of Wichita (later Wichita State University). O. W. wished to locate an evaluative instrument which could faithfully predict in a person the propensity to commit criminal acts. He found several professors who were anxious to assist him. Although the universities were never able to find or construct a reliable instrument, several sociologists were assigned to the Wichita Police Department for the purpose of assisting officers in redirecting wayward youths into productive activity.[51] Wilson ordered his staff to visit Wichita's schools and ask teachers to identify prospective delinquents. As delinquents and prospective delinquents came to the attention of the police, the officers were instructed by Wilson to "bring all the resources of the community to bear on the child in a subtle way." By this, Chief Wilson meant that officers assigned to crime prevention work were not to take punitive measures against young people, unless there was no other alternative. Instead, the child's personal situation should be investigated to determine if he or she was in need of food, clothing, shelter, parental guidance, vocational training, medical attention, dental care, spiritual aid, or other remedial assistance.[52] When a problem area was discovered, it was the investigating officer's job to ensure that the child in question received the help he or she needed. Wilson described the policeman's role as "an attempt to coordinate and direct the activity of other community activities." O. W. had some misgivings about the program, not because he thought that it was not a viable one, but because he questioned the desirability of the police doing work which was not generally considered to be in their realm. He confided to August Vollmer that he feared that his juvenile officers were "transgressing in the field of juvenile court probation officers."[53] Nevertheless, in the absence of affirmative action from Judge Hudson, and in the face of a shortage of probation officers, the chief decided to continue a program which he felt was productive. It would later prove to be a costly decision.

Other Wilsonian innovations were less dramatic than his experiment in "human engineering," though his penchant for change could be seen almost everywhere. In an effort to decrease punitive contacts between police officers and citizens he acted on the advice of his traffic lieutenant, Ray Ashworth, and purchased a small truck, installed a loudspeaker on it, and deployed it in areas of the city which had a high incidence of traffic accidents. The operator of the truck, usually Ashworth, would loudly call to the attention of errant drivers their violations. Traffic citations were issued only for serious infractions. A national magazine published an article on the concept.[54] Wilson also changed the policeman's uniform from the traditional blue to khaki. The uniforms were similar to army officer garb. O. W. felt they were more stylish, easier to maintain, and more appropriate to the semimilitary nature of the police service. In 1936, Chief Wilson had all his blue police cars painted white in an attempt to make them more visible to citizens.[55]

As O. W. Wilson's reputation as a reform police administrator spread, observers were drawn to Wichita to see his police department in action. Major articles in *Reader's Digest* and in *True Detective Mysteries*[56] told of his programs and innovations. He spent two months in Europe studying foreign police systems through a grant from the Oberlaender Trust. He served for five months as a visiting lecturer at Harvard University. When the government of Afghanistan sent six men abroad to study foreign police systems, two went to Scotland Yard, two went to the French Sûreté, and two went to Wichita. He was invited by the American Bar Association to speak on "making the police force an efficient fighting unit." The speech was broadcast nationally by the Columbia Broadcasting System.[57] Public administrators from across the country asked him to study their police departments and bring them in line with the Wichita model. He was unable to accept most of the invitations; however, he did direct reorganizational studies of several major police forces, one of the most noteworthy of which was the Dallas Police Department.[58] Requests from city managers and mayors to recommend men for chief of police positions almost always met with a favorable response from Wilson, as he placed his best command personnel in responsible jobs nationwide.[59] As a result of this national acclaim, O. W. was a regular participant in criminology conferences at major universities. It was at such a conference that he embarked on one of his boldest experiments.

During the spring of 1936, Wilson was attending a conference in Milwaukee when he met Edwin H. Sutherland, chairman of the Department of Sociology at Indiana University and one of America's most distinguished criminologists. Dr. Sutherland had for decades been a leading authority on crime and delinquency, and it was he who had first propounded the theory of "white collar crime." Sutherland had a brilliant graduate student named Hans Riemer. He though that Riemer had the potential to make a substantial contribution to the discipline of corrections, and he was guiding him toward a career in that field. Because Sutherland saw in Riemer highly developed qualities of scholarship, he hit on an idea to have his student actually incarcerated in prison to study first-hand an inmate culture. Unfortunately, the criminologist had been unable to find anyone in a position to implement his plan, until he met O. W. Wilson.

When O. W. was told of the idea, he felt that it had merit, and he decided to help. Wilson called Judge A. S. Foulk, executive secretary of the Kansas Board of Administration, and related the plan to him. Judge Foulk told the chief that the only way the idea could succeed was to process Riemer through the criminal justice system like any other offender. Chief Wilson devised an elaborate plan to simulate a crime. Captain Leroy Bowery and his secretary, Thayl Roth, were participants in the plan. Riemer came to Wichita under the alias of John Krafft. Using his alias, he issued a forged twenty-five dollar check to Miss Roth. When a local bank informed Miss Roth of the forgery, she signed a warrant for the arrest of John Krafft, and Bowery took him into custody. Krafft was transported to city jail, fingerprinted, and photographed. Two weeks later, he was tried by District Court Judge Robert L. NeSmith, who was unaware of the situation. Krafft was found guilty. The young graduate student was sentenced to a one-to-five year term in the Kansas State Prison.

Riemer spent three months in prison before he had completed his research. Judge Foulk then had him released and a pardon from Governor Alf Landon was issued. Since Riemer's fingerprints were on file with the FBI, O. W. Wilson wrote a letter to J. Edgar Hoover informing him of the facts of the case and asking the director to remove Riemer's fingerprints from federal files. Riemer went on to write several scholarly articles on his research, and he later became supervisor of correctional services for the Wisconsin Youth Services Division.[60]

That same year, the FBI's support of the Wichita Police Department disappeared. FBI agents who had been scheduled to teach in the Kansas League of Municipalities Police School never reported. Written communications from Wilson to FBI headquarters went unanswered. Pledges of technical assistance, such as consultation on a new fingerprint classification system, went unfulfilled. No evidence can be uncovered to determine whether or not O. W. Wilson ever knew precisely why Hoover decided to withdraw his support from Wilson's department, although O. W. was acutely aware of the fact that he had fallen out of favor with Hoover. Since Hoover did not usually confide in others why he invoked such sanctions, one can only speculate on the cause of that break. Certainly by 1936 O. W. had become something of a national celebrity for his reform efforts in Wichita, and Hoover often viewed innovative chiefs of police as competitors. He believed himself to be the patriarch of American law enforcement, and those who arose to challenge that position were often deprived of FBI support.[61] Although personal and professional jealousy may have been a major source of Hoover discontent, Wilson could have offended Hoover in other ways. For example, he once confided in August Vollmer that he was concerned that too much police power was being centralized in Washington, and that "such a police scheme was not intended by the founders of our constitution." He sensed that law enforcement was primarily a local responsibility, so "the Federal government should be left out of the picture."[62] In 1934, Wilson wrote an article which articulated this fear of federal intervention in local affairs. He asserted that effective crime control could be initiated only if the states were allowed to coordinate training, records, major investigations, and minimum standards for local police agencies, with the federal government serving merely as a clearinghouse for information. In this article was contained the first published argument for state-sponsored minimum entrance level and training standards in American police history.[63] Thus, Wilson's action in the Riemer case, his rise to prominence as a leading police administrator, his advocacy of local control of law enforcement and his opposition to federal police power, all could have contributed to the break with Hoover. At least one authority has written that the split occurred during the 1950's or 1960's, but it is clear that it happened in 1936.[64] J. Edgar Hoover's animosity was first generated during Wilson's Wichita years, but it was to remain in force throughout O. W.'s career. In Chicago, thirty years later, Director Hoover would provide Wilson with no more FBI aid than he had in Wichita. It was a situation which consistently troubled Wilson.

Many of O. W. Wilson's most innovative programs in Wichita involved educational institutions. He had learned from August Vollmer the value in making maximum use of a local university. Indeed, Wilson had involved both of Wichita's universities in his crime prevention program, and he had recruited students from both campuses to police work. Chief Wilson, however, sought a way to strengthen and formalize the relationship between the Municipal University of Wichita and the Wichita Police Department. Thus far, no one had adequately defined what the relationship between education and law enforcement should be. Since there were but few institutions which had even attempted to insert in the regular curriculum police administration coursework, Wilson did not have a philosophical foundation on which to base any educational plan. In fact, he was not yet sure that police administration as a discipline was worthy of academic status.[65] O. W. had become convinced long ago that education was a necessary element in the movement to professionalize the police; nevertheless, he was not sure whether specialized training or liberal arts education were in order. He anguished over the issue before arriving at a decision. O. W. typed the major aspects of a policeman's job. From his list, he eliminated low-level skills, tasks which could be best taught by a police department or a training academy, and subjects which could not achieve a degree of academic respectability among professors. From those tasks remaining he constructed seven courses: criminal law, personal identification, police patrol practices, criminal evidence, traffic control, criminal investigation, and police administration.[66] Wilson then identified political science as the academic discipline having the closest relationship to police science. He discussed his idea with Dr. Hugo Wall, Chairman of the Department of Political Science, and it was decided that the seven police science courses would be added to the political science curriculum as an area of specialization.

The university curriculum committee formally approved of the plan, and it was implemented in 1936. Chief Wilson was placed in charge of the police science students. O. W. also appointed instructors for each course, though he reserved police administration for himself.[67] Once the new curriculum had been installed, Wilson then turned his attention to the matter of enticing the best students into service with the Wichita Police Department. The financial hardship which Wilson had experienced during his undergraduate days led to an idea that was to assist the police department in its recruiting efforts.

Wilson recalled his days as a Berkeley patrolman. Although there had not been a serious depression at that time, his father's financial reversal had placed on him the same pressures that university students of 1936 were laboring under. He remembered the difficulties he had experienced working full-time and carrying a heavy schedule of classes. O. W. sensed that if a young man could work on a part-time basis and attend school with a reduced course load, he could continue his education, gain experience in his chosen career field, and achieve a degree of financial independence. Accordingly, O. W. Wilson initiated America's first police cadet program. Carefully selected police science students, carrying a twelve-hour academic load, were put to work as paid Wichita police officers four hours a day. The selection procedures, duties, and uniforms were the same for cadets as they were for regular officers. The major stipulations for cadets were that they had to be at least twenty-one years of age, and in their junior year.[68]

Chief Wilson implemented a six-week recruit training academy for cadets. He held it biannually, once in the winter and once in the summer, so it would coincide with breaks in the academic calendar. The chief did not wish to be responsible for his cadets' falling behind in their studies.[69] Wilson's training regimen was so gruelling that Dr. Wall termed it "unduly severe." A typical cadet's training day began with classes in technical law enforcement subjects at police headquarters from 8:00 A.M. to noon. After a half hour for lunch, firearms and physical training lasted until 3:00 P.M., followed by a three-hour liberty. From 6:00 P.M. until midnight cadets were assigned to patrol duty with a veteran officer. They worked a six-day week, with Sunday off. The six weeks mercifully ended the weekend before the university's academic quarter began. Cadets found university life and a mere four-hour work day a welcome respite from O. W. Wilson's training academy.[70]

Chief Wilson personally interviewed all candidates for police cadet positions. Joe Stone, a former Wichita cadet, recalls that Wilson was a formidable figure to a young police hopeful. Stern appearing and erect, "with eyes that looked right through you," the chief would brusquely ask why the interviewee would make a good officer. In Joe Stone's case, Wilson pointed out that he was a rather frail young man for such a demanding job. Young Stone explained that in addition to attending school, he had been working three jobs to make ends meet. Stone promised that he would add to his weight of 148 pounds if he could reduce his schedule to one job. Joe was startled when Wilson's placid expression changed to a grin, followed by robust laughter. The chief informed Stone that he was hired. Only after Stone had completed the six weeks training course did he understand why Wilson had laughed at his comment, for by that time the young cadet's weight had dropped to 132 pounds.

Joe Stone, like most cadets, eventually became a regular Wichita police officer. When the police department did not have enough openings to employ cadets as regular policemen, Chief Wilson would place them with other agencies, such as the Kansas State Highway Patrol. He did this rather than risk losing good men to another profession. As a result of his propensity to place Wichita police officers with other departments, both as patrolmen and chiefs, the department soon earned the title of "the West Point of Law Enforcement."[71]

Wilson's major reorganization plans had been completed, and the department appeared to be functioning smoothly; he now turned his attention to the intricacies of personnel administration. He questioned the traditional way in which officers were rated for their performance. To evaluate them on the basis of arrests made or traffic citations issued was not, in Wilson's view, an accurate measure of productivity. He drafted a form on which were placed fifteen traits deemed desirable in officers: reliability, judgment, industry, initiative, energy, observation, persistence, sources of information, enthusiasm, memory, physical courage, learning ability, decisiveness, confidence, and communication skill. Wilson assigned weights to each trait, installed a grading system, and evaluated his officers annually.[72]

Now that the department had an evaluative system, it became obvious to O. W. that he should reinforce it with a method of rewarding above-average officers who, because of limited promotional opportunities, were destined to remain patrolmen or sergeants throughout their careers. In municipal law enforcement, one qualified for a pay increase when promoted, or when the legislative body granted all workers a cost-of-living adjustment. Chief Wilson worked out a system of graduated pay, whereby officers in each classification had five pay steps. Increases could be received only after an above-average annual evaluation. August Vollmer recommended that he abandon the idea, but Wilson would not. Unfortunately, the city manager could not get the concept funded. Thirty years later, the graduated pay system attained universal acceptance in law enforcement.[73]

Wilson was also troubled by the absence of a reliable instrument to measure a man's leadership ability. Police promotions were often based upon an officer's work in an assignment which was only partially related to the promotional vacancy. Wilson studied methods of predicting leadership capabilities, including the role of various blood groupings and glandular functions as factors in determining the traits of leadership.[74] His research did not lead to fruitful results.

By 1938, O. W. Wilson's aggressive enforcement of vice laws had alienated a number of influential citizens. He had driven bootleggers out of Wichita, and his orders to "suppress, imprison, and drive prostitutes from the city" had been taken literally by vice officers. Bath houses frequented by local businessmen were constantly being closed down as houses of prostitution. Wichita's downtown area had been blighted by the Depression, so that prostitutes were often welcomed into rooming houses which had a high vacancy rate. Prostitutes paid a higher rent and were more dependable than other residents, making them valuable occupants to the businessmen who owned these otherwise unprofitable buildings. As Wilson drove the prostitutes from Wichita he antagonized many of the city's landlords. It was not that the chief was morally opposed to prostitution. In fact, he favored legalizing it and placing it under government control.[75] Nevertheless, as long as prostitution was a violation of state law, Wilson felt that he had an obligation to smash it, which he consistently did. Wilson's enemies had grown over the years, but they had been afraid to act in the face of his enormous popularity in the community. Then, an incident occurred which furnished them with the courage to rid themselves of their formidable adversary.

Juvenile Court Judge Clyde Hudson had been content to allow Wilson's crime prevention program to continue, for the judge felt it to be a political asset as long as he could take credit for it in speeches before Wichita's civic clubs. But when the program's success became more closely associated with O. W. Wilson than with him, the judge grew concerned that he was being left out of the spotlight of publicity. Now that the program had proved its worth, Hudson decided to take it over, but in such a way that his motives could not be impugned. He knew that the juvenile court was the only public agency with the statutory authority to adjudicate and refer juveniles to community agencies. Wilson had indeed usurped the juvenile court's prerogative, but with Judge Hudson's blessing. The judge called the Wichita city attorney and requested him to seek a legal opinion from the state attorney general. The attorney general ruled that the police department had no legal right to form a juvenile division, and it must disband the unit in order to be consistent with law.[76] Wilson condemned the opinion, but the damage had been done.

Two city commissioners, Robert Israel and Schuyler Crawford, represented those forces in the community who wished to see Wilson removed from office.[77] Using the attorney general's opinion as a lever, they criticized the chief for wasting tax money on frivolous programs, for operating a training school for police chiefs, and for having too many personnel for a city the size of Wichita. They persuaded other commissioners to cut $18,000 from the police operating budget, forcing Wilson to curtail many of his specialized programs. City Manager Bert Wells, who had always been O. W.'s advocate, was accused of slovenly administration by Israel and Crawford. Wells was so preoccupied with his own defense that he was effectively neutralized as Wilson's spokesman. In the midst of the controversy, Wells resigned. He had been with the city for twenty-five years, and decided that he had fought his final battle.[78]

As word spread of the attempt to force Wilson out as chief of police, community groups rallied to his support. O. W. knew that the community was for him, but to him "it looked like a losing battle." Even if he remained in Wichita, an unresponsive city commission could, through fiscal sanctions, force him to cut back on programs and personnel drastically. He decided to "adopt a policy of watchful waiting."[79]

Wilson's situation was complicated by a disloyal subordinate, Captain Leroy Bowery, who saw in the crisis an opportunity to become chief of police. Bowery became the "commissioners' man." He brought intelligence information to them, while attempting to undercut Wilson's authority with his officers. Furthermore, Bowery refused to join Wilson in defending his crime prevention unit.

Over two hundred citizens filled city commission chambers to protest what the *Wichita Eagle* termed the "sinister force" attempting to drive Wilson from Wichita. Citizens whom O. W. had never met spoke in his behalf. The president of Wichita's Council of Churches expressed confidence in Wilson, along with the presidents of the Chamber of Commerce, the Stearman Aircraft Corporation, the school board, the county bar association, the Kiwanis Club, the Rotary Club, the Civitan Club, the Exchange Club, the Commonwealth Club, and the Lions Club. Dozens of local physicians, attorneys, and merchants also supported Chief Wilson, who was moved by the vote of confidence.[80] It also impressed him with "the value of the hours of hard work we had spent establishing proper public relations."[81]

It soon became clear to Wilson that he could not serve a legislative body which would not totally support his efforts. He wrote Vollmer:

> The situation here is an intolerable one, and the sooner I get out the better it will be for me. I see no possibility of this situation working itself out. I can anticipate some rough weather ahead if I attempt to stay in the boat.[82]

Any doubt O. W. might have had about leaving was quickly dispelled. Commissioners Israel and Crawford summoned the chief to a private meeting to discuss his future with the city. During the course of the conference Wilson was threatened with a series of unpleasant alternatives should he choose to remain in office. In a letter to August Vollmer, Wilson listed the tactics the commissioners said they would use to discredit him:

1. Have my salary slashed.
2. Have the commission order the discontinuance of certain police activities, such as the maintenance of records.
3. The appointment of a disloyal subordinate officer as assistant chief, with complete control over police personnel.
4. Appointment of the same man as Director of Public Safety over police and fire.
5. An investigation of the department with a view of raising sufficient stench to justify ordering my suspension and leaving me simmering on the pan without salary until I was tired out.[83]

Wilson decided to leave Wichita on 15 May 1939. Instead of castigating his adversaries, he again met with the commission in private to work out a way of resigning which would not leave the community in a turmoil. O. W. planned to leave "as nearly like a gentleman as I know how, without any ill will toward anyone in the community." It was agreed that Wilson would be given a one-year leave of absence to serve as a consultant to the Public Administration Service in Chicago. He had been invited to do so by Director Donald Stone. It was understood that Wilson would formally submit his resignation several months after he had left Wichita, but that he would make it clear to the community that "the leave of absence was bona fide."[84]

O. W. Wilson said good-bye to the many friends he had made in Wichita. He assembled his officers for a last crab meeting and thanked them for their cooperation in making the department the best of its type anywhere. Following his brief address, Captain "Tex" Ingram lectured the assemblage on the meaning of loyalty, a message which was meant for Leroy Bowery.[85] In characteristic spartan style, Wilson wired August Vollmer: "Have years leave. Will be with Don Stone in Chicago."[86]

6

THE WAR YEARS

O. W. Wilson left Wichita firmly convinced that the primary obstacle to police reform was the influence of partisan politics on police administration. His initial experience in Fullerton, coupled with the Wichita situation, persuaded him that progressive chiefs of police could not effectively serve unless they were freed from the corrupting impact of politics.[1] He was to decry political influence on law enforcement in his future writings and lectures, and more than two decades hence was to go to extraordinary lengths to insulate himself from it when he assumed the superintendency of the Chicago Police Department.

The Wilsons arrived in Chicago after a three-day drive from Wichita. They spent one week in a downtown hotel, relaxing and renewing old acquaintances. Vernis located a furnished apartment which O. W. found quite satisfactory. He wrote August Vollmer that:

> We have an extra bedroom in our apartment and if you and Pat come this way be sure and plan on spending the night with us. You will be pleased to know that the apartment does not possess a piano so your rest will not be disturbed, at least by any musical performance.[2]

Following his brief vacation, Wilson plunged into work. His job with the Public Administration Service was two-fold: to survey municipal police departments and recommend plans for reorganization, and to write monographs on various aspects of police administration. He and a former Wichita subordinate, Theo Hall, had already done considerable work on a statistical analysis of the deployment of patrol cars in a community. Consequently, his first monograph for PAS was a study which set forth a method for the chronological and geographical distribution of a patrol force in medium-sized cities, based on statistical predictions of serious crimes. Eliot Ness, Director of Public Safety in Cleveland, praised the study for being "of outstanding importance and value to every police administrator."[3] He went on to say that "for the first time police officials have a reliable standard with which to measure the effectiveness of the distribution of their respective forces."[4] On the basis of this study, Wilson concluded that one-man patrol cars were indeed more efficient than two-man cars. This study was to form the statistical foundation for his campaign to convince the police establishment that they should modify their manning patterns.

O. W. Wilson was assigned to survey the police departments in Peoria, Illinois; Hartford, Connecticut; Huntington, West Virginia; and San Antonio, Texas. He was not surprised to find that the political environment in most of these cities was similar to the one he had left in Wichita. He wrote August Vollmer that "the Peoria situation was a pitiful one. To reorganize that police department and place it on a sound operating basis would be a source of considerable gratification."[5] Perhaps Wilson's most challenging survey was in San Antonio, where he was given virtual *carte blanche* to mold the department into a professional police force. In addition to reorganizing the department, O. W. was encouraged to identify and recommend men for promotion to key positions. He selected the department's entire command staff, including the chief of police. Not surprisingly, the new chief was Ray Ashworth, who had been one of his most trusted subordinates in Wichita. Wilson spent almost a month in San Antonio, during which he became almost completely occupied with the survey. Unbeknownst to O. W., however, there was a plan being formulated to bring him to the University of California at Berkeley as a professor of police administration.

August Vollmer had been lecturing at the University of California since 1931, where he taught a series of police administration courses which had been added to the political science curriculum.[6] In 1939 a university committee recommended an expansion of the program and the hiring of a full-time faculty member to administer it. That year, Professor A. M. Kidd of the law school sent a memorandum to George D. Louderback of the College of Arts and Letters recommending an expansion of the police program into a full major. In the memorandum, Professor Kidd listed, in order of preference, ten men whom he thought should be interviewed for the directorship. O. W. Wilson was the first name on the list, but Kidd held little hope of recruiting Wilson as long as he was chief of police in Wichita.[7] When O. W. left Wichita, the university, through August Vollmer, David P. Barrows, Chairman of the Political

Science Department, and President Robert G. Sproul, set out to attract him to the university.

August Vollmer felt that the Berkeley professorship would only be accepted by Wilson if the university would go to extraordinary lengths to make it attractive. Vollmer knew that O. W. would never be content merely to teach and conduct research. Wilson's love was law enforcement, and he would not permit himself to be isolated from the workaday world of police administration. He had to be given freedom to pursue his goal of police professionalization. The tactic was to offer O. W. a prestigious position, at top salary, with freedom to engage in outside consultative activities, and with a reduced teaching load. Vollmer sent several letters to Wilson informing him of the professorship, and when he received no unfavorable reply from O. W., Barrows and Sproul formally offered Wilson the post.

President Sproul offered O. W. Wilson a tenured position as full professor of police administration at an annual salary of $6,000, with moving expenses of $500. In addition, he was promised summers off to pursue consultative activities, and promised operating independence in molding the academic program into shape. Barrows followed up the offer with a letter assigning Wilson a load of two courses per semester, rather than the customary three, while repeating Sproul's pledge of autonomy. O. W. Wilson accepted the position on 24 July 1939, thereby becoming America's first fulltime professor of police administration.[8]

Wilson resigned from the Public Administration Service on 12 August 1939, approximately three months after he had taken the job. Because of the arrangements which had been made with the university, he continued on with PAS in a temporary capacity, writing monographs and conducting police reorganizational surveys during summer vacations and semester breaks.[9] Over the next twenty years, he was to complete administrative surveys for dozens of major police departments, and place as police administrators more than one hundred former subordinates and students.

O. W. took the occasion of his move to California to formally terminate his leave of absence from the Wichita Police Department. In a letter to the new city manager, Wilson formalized the resignation which city officials knew would come, but which was unexpected by many members of the community. Wilson tersely informed the manager:

> In view of the permanent character of my appointment to the University of California, I consider it wise to submit my resignation to you.[10]

With this letter, O. W. Wilson's formal ties to the Wichita Police

Department were severed. He did not formally notify members of the department of his resignation; this was the city manager's job. He did remain in contact with many of his former Wichita subordinates.

O. W., Vernis and Henry relocated in Berkeley during the summer of 1939. On 7 January 1940, Vernis gave birth to their second child, Sally Jo. The following year, the Wilsons abandoned their marriage of eighteen years. Vernis was experiencing deep emotional problems which had led her to alcoholism. The Wilsons legally separated in 1942, and were divorced the following year. Vernis moved to Los Angeles to live with her mother. In 1948, Vernis Haddon Wilson died from an overdose of sleeping tablets.[11]

During his initial year at Berkeley, Wilson began work on his first major publication. At the behest of the International City Managers' Association, Professor Wilson wrote and edited one of the first American textbooks on police administration. The book, entitled *Municipal Police Administration* was originally published as a mimeographed manual in 1938; however, it was released as a textbook in 1943. The text became something of a classic in law enforcement. By 1970, it had sold over 100,000 copies and had been revised seven times, though it generally remained consistent with its original structure.[12] Wilson contributed to all but the last two editions.

O. W. had both short-term and long-range plans for the academic program at the University of California. He wished to make his program acceptable to police practitioners, while retaining respectability in the academic community. To achieve this, Wilson set out to make the program practical, by offering coursework designed to prepare police students for administrative positions with law enforcement agencies, but scholarly, by utilizing criminological, medical, and psychiatric research data on crime, delinquency, and deviance. He began by drafting a core of courses to satisfy an undergraduate concentration in political science. Since Wilson wished to guide his program toward autonomy, with its own faculty and degree, he took a first step in that direction by having the police administration program designated as a "bureau" within the Political Science Department. President Robert Sproul was instrumental in this change. Sproul was a great admirer of Wilson and a champion of the program. He was to actively support all of O. W. Wilson's efforts to expand the program.[13]

With the outbreak of World War II, many of the activities at the University of California were curtailed as both students and professors entered the armed services. Wilson decided to enlist in the army, even though he was well beyond draft age. Because of his age, however, he needed the assistance of influential friends.

Joe Harris, a former Berkeley professor of political science and now a

U. S. Army colonel, learned that the army was beginning the School of Military Government in Charlottesville, Virginia. The purpose of the school was to train carefully selected officers to assist in the reestablishment of civil government services in liberated countries. The army had authorized the recruitment of fifty majors and lieutenant colonels, who would attend the school, then serve in the European theatre. Harris urged Wilson to apply for one of the commissions.[14]

O. W. completed an application for an army commission, to which he attached a four-page supplemental statement informing the army of his extensive police experience, including his publications and consultancies.[15] Wilson knew that his department chairman, David P. Barrows, was a retired army major general who was on friendly terms with the commander of the School of Military Government. He prevailed on Barrows to write a letter of recommendation in his behalf. In it, Barrows described Wilson as a man "who lacks nothing," and recommended him "very heartily, and without reservation." Donald Stone wrote a letter of reference in which he termed O. W. "one of the outstanding, if not the foremost, expert in municipal police adminstration in the United States."[16] On 10 January 1943, O. W. Wilson was accepted into the United States Army with the rank of lieutenant colonel. He was assigned to the School of Military Government, Charlottesville, Virginia.

Enroute to Charlottesville, O. W. stopped to see friends in Los Angeles, Wichita, and Chicago. He arrived at the school in late January and became immersed in his studies, which consisted primarily of an introduction to army service and an orientation to foreign systems of government. The curriculum was challenging. Students worked nine-hour days, took daily quizzes, and taught seminars in their areas of specialization. As O. W. was the only officer with law enforcement experience, he was kept busy lecturing his colleagues on the nature of public safety administration. Wilson wrote Vollmer that the quality of the school and its students "exceeded my expectations."

There was little to do during off-duty hours except study. Adult recreation facilities were almost nonexistent. Wilson was pleased when Mrs. Vollmer regularly sent him bottles of Scotch.[17] Army records indicate that he graduated from the school with honors on 11 May 1943 and remained in Charlottesville as a public safety instructor until August.

In the fall of 1943, Colonel Wilson was assigned to Naples as Director of Public Safety for the military government. His job was to help rebuild the carabinieri into an effective law enforcement agency and direct the customs police.[18] He stayed in Naples for approximately three months, following which he was transferred to England to prepare for a mission which the Allied Command felt was of critical importance.

Wilson was assigned to a military government team consisting of both American and British officers, whose task was to plan for the eventual occupation of France and Germany. O. W. was Director of the Public Safety Division, German Country Unit, Supreme Headquarters of the Allied Expeditionary Force (SHAEF).[19] His division was basically a planning staff whose objectives were to write procedures for reinstating vital public safety functions in Germany and identifying Germans who had been active members of the Nazi party. High-level Nazis were to be prohibited from holding responsible government offices.

British intelligence had a number of books on the German police. Wilson studied them closely for information which would assist him in drafting a reorganizational plan. He discovered that before the war, law enforcement had been primarily a local responsibility, but that when Hitler came to power he centralized control and added two new branches, the Gestapo and the Security Police. To Wilson, this was odious. He decided that it should be a first priority to reinitiate local control of law enforcement, preferably through the states, and eliminate any semblance of a secret police. All plans for German law enforcement were grounded on the premise that the police would be locally controlled.

Since Wilson and his staff had the responsibility of rebuilding the German police from the bottom up, he ordered his subordinates to conduct studies on a multiplicity of problems and issues. Should, for example, the police be rearmed, and if so when? Should they be initially given full arrest powers? Should the criminal courts be given full responsibility for administering the law? The staff recommended a comprehensive program of police reform. The policy on German public safety reorganization was drafted by O. W. Wilson into a massive volume entitled *Public Safety Manual*. It became the master plan for rebuilding a defeated nation's entire public safety apparatus.

Insofar as de-Nazification was concerned, Colonel Wilson took extra care to surround himself with superior men. He appointed Captain Minor Keith Wilson director of de-Nazification activities.[20] He found Milton Chernin, former dean of the School of Social Welfare at Berkeley, doing menial tasks as an enlisted man in London and had him assigned to the staff with a second lieutenant's commission. Several former Wichita subordinates, notably Theo Hall, Ray Ashworth, and Neil Anderson, were all put to work. Together, this team, led by Wilson, devised a systematic method of de-Nazification.[21]

As the allied armies occupied Germany, Wilson's Public Safety Division moved to Berlin. Its first priority was to screen the German population for past Nazi activities, for it would be impossible to restore the government until Nazi zealots could be identified and prohibited from holding office. Keith Wilson devised a three-page questionnaire which all applicants for government positions were ordered to complete. The form was made up of questions designed to trace a person's activities during the War.[22] Extensive background investigations were undertaken to check the accuracy of the data on the completed questionnaires. O. W. found that the German army had kept elaborate records. Great masses of information had been collected on citizens by the Gestapo, who had been ordered to destroy these records during the fall of Berlin but for inexplicable reasons had not. As a consequence, Wilson had a wealth of information at his disposal with which to evaluate citizens who applied for government service.

Upon entering Berlin, Wilson did not know what to expect from the civilian population. There was even a rumor that a cadre of hard core Nazis would go underground to engage in guerrilla warfare. For a time, O. W. considered fingerprinting approximately three million Germans and issuing them identity cards. This seemingly monumental task left Wilson open to attack in later years, as critics in Chicago used it as an example of Wilson's muddled approach to problem solving. Actually, O. W. did initiate a staff study on the idea, but he abandoned it after he found the concept unworkable and unnecessary. The charge that he intended to pursue the plan until ordered not to do so by higher authority is clearly refuted in a letter to August Vollmer in which Wilson confided to the chief that it would take four thousand Americans to complete the project and "there is serious doubt in my mind that the results obtained in the deterrence of underground activities would justify such an expenditure of manpower."[23] Wilson finally aborted the idea when a French resistance leader informed him that his covert activities during the war would not have been hindered in the slightest by such action. So, the idea was Wilson's, as was the decision to abandon it. O. W. Wilson never abandoned or adopted a concept until he had fully evaluated it. This specific criticism of him was contrived and misleading.

Wilson set up investigative components in German communities whose function was to conduct background evaluations on applicants for government jobs. O. W. hit upon the idea of staffing these "special branches," as they were called, with German Jews, who could be counted on to faithfully conduct such investigations.[24]

Colonel Wilson's de-Nazification plan did not prohibit all Nazis from serving in the government. So called "nominal Nazis," those citizens who were members, but who were not really Nazis in spirit, were allowed to hold office. Wilson discovered that many professional groups, such as physicians and teachers, were forced to join the party in order to practice their callings. Consequently, he persuaded his commanding general to adopt the "nominal Nazi" typology so that people with perfunctory party affiliation would not be penalized for life. Unfortunately, some of the army's field commanders, who had the responsibility for translating de-Nazification policy into action, did not share this humanitarian view. Many of these commanders had been combat soldiers, so they systematically eliminated from consideration Germans who had even nominal affiliation with the Nazi party. Wilson spent a great deal of time in the field asking commanders to adhere to the policy.[25] Just when de-Nazification began to run smoothly, an incident occurred which prompted a dramatic modification in the plan.

General George Patton had been appointed military governor of Bavaria. During the course of an interview, General Patton compared the Nazi party with the Republicans and Democrats, thereby causing a furor. General Eisenhower was furious. He relieved Patton of his duties and ordered him home. General Lucius Clay, O. W. Wilson's superior, decided that something drastic had to be done to impress upon the American public that its army was not soft on Nazis. Without consulting his staff, Clay issued a directive which was entitled "Law No. 8." The directive prohibited former members of the Nazi party from holding any government position above common laborer. Wilson was appalled. The law was unworkable, since many of the country's most talented individuals had been inactive party members. Colonel Wilson did not try to talk Clay out of pursuing his plan, however. Lucius Clay was the general, so Wilson felt that he had an obligation to support Law No. 8, despite its flaws.[26]

Almost from its inception, Law No. 8 was doomed to failure. Soon after its passage, General Clay realized it was unworkable, but he would not countermand the order, for to do so would mean a loss of face. Instead, he sought to dilute the law's effect by appointing local review boards, staffed by German citizens, to administer it. These boards promptly ignored Law No. 8, and "nominal Nazis" were again allowed to become government employees.[27]

Unlike de-Nazification, law enforcement in Germany never became a major political issue. O. W. was given an almost free hand to reorganize the police as he saw fit. His initial reservations about rearming policemen and granting them full police authority were based upon a scenario that to do so could lead them to become a paramilitary German resistance movement. It soon became clear to Colonel Wilson that police officers, who were carefully recruited, had no interest in such activity.

Wilson found that his new policemen were a dedicated lot, committed to public service. Accordingly, he allowed them to have more and more power and authority, until they were eventually armed and permitted to engaged in the full range of law enforcement activities, a radical departure from the early days of occupation when they were allowed only to direct traffic and maintain order.[28]

Wilson admired the German police. They had a penchant for organization, carried out their duties professionally, enforced the law evenly, and had a love of formal training. On this last point, O. W. discovered that his policemen were starved for training. He instituted a system of pre-service, in-service, and specialized training designed to professionalize law enforcement officers at all levels. Colonel Wilson could not bear to see an ill-trained police officer, even in a foreign country, and so he set out in earnest to correct this deficiency.

O. W. Wilson was promoted to full colonel in 1945, and the following year was awarded the Bronze Star and the Legion of Merit. An excerpt from the citation for the Legion of Merit follows:

> Colonel Wilson initiated extensive research and prepared, coordinated with other allies and implemented projects of the utmost significance in the future supervision of a vanquished country. The plans, in the building of which he played such a major role, were noteworthy for their qualities of completeness, precision and thoroughness.

A passage from the Bronze Star citation praised Wilson:

> ... for meritorious service in connection with military operations. ... Colonel Wilson fulfilled with marked initiative and good judgment the writing of the Public Safety Manual and of preparing Public Safety Forms for use in Germany. ... Colonel Wilson also assisted materially in the procurement and assignment of public safety personnel in liberated countries and in Germany, thereby contributing in no small part to the success of civil affairs and military government on the European continent.

In 1946, a decision was made to civilianize the military government contingent. O. W. Wilson was given the choice of either a discharge or a transfer to a civilian position with the federal government. If he chose the latter alternative, he would serve one more year in Germany, performing the same duties he had been assigned in the army. Wilson was aware that the University of California was anxiously awaiting his return but felt that his job in Germany had not been completed. He decided to remain in Europe for another year. President Sproul was notified, and he agreed to hold Wilson's position open until the fall semester of 1947.[29]

Wilson spent much of his last year in Civil Affairs, recruiting staff to upgrade the German police. He was disappointed when the military turned down a request to have August Vollmer appointed as his aide. Vollmer was of advanced age and in poor physical condition, but Wilson believed that Vollmer at his worst was still the best available man for the job.[30]

By the spring of 1947, O. W. prepared to return home. He decided to set aside two months for travel to England, Belgium, and France to study their police systems. With typical Wilsonian logic he confided in Vollmer that his European tour of duty would not have been wisely spent if he did not collect a mass of police data to pass on to his students.[31] Later that summer, O. W. returned to Berkeley to resume his duties as professor of police administration.

Wilson's army experience furnished him with a number of ideas which he would employ throughout his career. It also reinforced many concepts he had used before his army service. O. W. had long been convinced of the need for police departments to be precisely organized according to some logical plan. The military system of organization and administration strongly appealed to him. He adopted and adapted many army organizational concepts. Wilson believed that commanding officers, all the way down to line supervisors, must have small spans of control. A rigid chain of command was essential to exercise organizational control. Top commanders should unilaterally articulate policy, and rule by fiat. Strict discipline must be enforced on all personnel, with quick, decisive action taken against offenders. Specialization by task was desirable. Continuing training of line officers must be carried out. Line units must be well equipped and highly mobile. Advanced communication equipment was needed to link field units with headquarters. These, then, were to form a basis for the way in which professional police departments should be organized, according to Wilson.

In his view, law enforcement should be organized along semimilitary lines. It was a philosophy which assumed that major structural reform of police agencies would ensure a change in institutitional values. Thus, pride would be developed in the ranks, honesty and integrity would naturally follow, and the quality of police service would ultimately be improved. It also assumed that patrolmen had nothing to offer the organization but their work. They had neither the right nor the responsibility to question orders from higher authority, or to participate in the policy formulation process. These concepts have been widely accepted in police administration, primarily because of the writings, teachings, and example of their champion, Orlando W. Wilson, who was convinced that a nation of police departments, organized and administered along Wilsonian lines, would ultimately lead to police professionalization. In effect, the dominant organizational strategy of the Wilsonian school of police administration was to organize an agency according to the military model, then place in command a scrupulously honest martinet, who ideally operated free of political oversight. Wilson would go to his grave convinced of the wisdom of this plan.

7

RETURN TO BERKELEY

The years immediately following O. W. Wilson's release from government service were largely devoted to two major projects: expansion of the Bureau of Police Administration to a full School of Criminology, and the writing of a textbook on police administration.

Much of the preliminary details aimed at broadening the police administration approach to criminology, and expanding the academic program to a full school had been worked out by August Vollmer prior to Wilson's return to Berkeley. Vollmer was widely respected by university officials, and the traditional university red tape which often accompanied curriculum revision had been avoided because of Vollmer's close personal relationship with President Robert Sproul. Sproul was a supporter of the criminology program. It was destined to prosper during his tenure.[1]

The criminology approach to education which would be employed by O. W. Wilson was a departure from past orthodoxy. It did not focus exclusively on one segment of the criminal justice system, such as police administration, corrections, or law. Instead, it took a systemic approach to education by introducing students to the broad system of criminal justice while allowing them to concentrate on coursework specifically applicable to their career orientation. In effect, students were expected to master a specialized curriculum in either law enforcement, corrections, or criminalistics, but were also required to take a core of criminology courses designed to acquaint them with the broad criminal justice field and with the function of justice agencies different from the ones in which they would some day work. For example, police students were required to take courses in corrections, and corrections students took coursework in police administration. Both students took courses in law, crime prevention, and the psychological aspects of criminology.[2] The Berkeley criminology curriculum was the forerunner of criminal justice education in American colleges and universities which was not to come into vogue for some two decades.

O. W. Wilson was not a traditional academician. He had no graduate degree, and had never published a scholarly article in an academic journal. Nevertheless, when in 1950 the Bureau of Police Administration became the School of Criminology, O. W. was appointed dean, based upon his preeminence in law enforcement.[3]

Wilson was a practical man. He did not intend to exclude theory and philosophy from the School of Criminology; however, it would be subordinated in importance to more practical undertakings. He was an educator, but his primary loyalty was to the field of law enforcement, which he wished to professionalize. O. W. would exhibit this higher loyalty by initiating a professional, rather than an academic curriculum. Although the school also offered a master's program in criminology, it, too, was a professional degree.[4] Graduates from Berkeley would eventually form the vanguard of the police professionalization movement which came to fruition in the late 1960's.

Since Wilson had founded a professional school, he set about to recruit a faculty which had distinguished itself in the field. Publications, teaching experience, and advanced degrees were not major criteria in Wilson's mind. He was interested almost exclusively in professional accomplishments.[5] The faculty Dean Wilson recruited reflected this posture. He selected Austin H. MacCormick as his corrections specialist. MacCormick had been an assistant director of the Federal Bureau of Prisons and had won a reputation as a progressive penal reformer during his seven years as commissioner of corrections for New York City. Douglas Kelley, former Director of the San Francisco County Psychopathic Hospital, was appointed a full professor of criminology. Paul Kirk, who had invented the term *criminalistics,* was hired to teach his specialty. He was assisted by M. Edwin O'Neill, who had been previously associated with the Chicago Police Department crime laboratory. John D. Holstrom, Berkeley chief of police, as well as several other local police officials, were appointed as lecturers. Only Kirk possessed the Ph.D. degree. The absence of doctoral degrees and traditional academic credentials in the School of Criminology would later become an issue, but not during Robert Sproul's tenure as president.

Wilson had compiled a massive amount of material on law enforcement dating back to his Wichita years and spanning his army service. From this data, he began writing a text on police administration. When completed in the summer of 1949, the book admirably mirrored his philosophy.

Spartan in style, the underlying themes were the need for personal and institutional integrity, independence from political domination, the military model of organization, progressive methods of crime detection, the scientific deployment of personnel, and on-going programs of community relations. In addition, Wilson extolled the virtues of his one-man car concept. He signed a contract with the McGraw-Hill Book Company in 1949, and the text was published the following year. By 1972, the book, by then in its third edition, had been translated into five languages and had outsold every other text offered by McGraw-Hill's college division,[6] despite its narrow subject matter and the sparsity of police administration programs in colleges and universities. By 1974, *Police Administration* had sold approximately 200,000 copies.[7]

In the classroom, Dean Wilson was a demanding professor. He did not usually require research papers, but his examinations were challenging. Wilson was not a particularly inspiring lecturer. He spoke in a monotone, mechanically, and without histrionics. He knew he had valuable information to share, and he employed no flamboyancy in the process. He maintained a formal relationship with students. The Dean felt it was undignified to fraternize with students, so he remained detached. Even those privileged few graduate students who were invited to his home for occasional seminars found that their professor had a wealth of data, but was aloof.[8] Nevertheless, O. W. Wilson did have a close relationship with one student.

Wilson's second wife was a former student. She entered the University of California at a mature age, following a divorce. Although she was a criminology major who during her undergraduate career had taken several courses from him, their romance did not bloom until after she had graduated. They were married in the fall of 1950. Three years later, Ruth Elinor Wilson gave birth to their only child, Patricia Anne.[9]

Ruth was a bright, articulate woman, with a clearcut sense of social position. She respected her husband, though they often took opposing positions on many of the social issues of the day. Ruth generally conformed to a liberal ideology, while O. W. subscribed to conservative values. For example, O. W. held the view that communism was responsible for much of the nation's ills, while Ruth strongly resisted the notion.[10] Disagreements occasionally erupted into heated arguments. Nevertheless, although the marriage experienced its share of rough spots, Ruth filled a need in O. W.'s life by challenging him, prodding, sympathizing, and tending to his needs, while granting him the privacy which he craved from time to time.

During the early 1950's, a U. S. Senate select committee, chaired by Estes Kefauver of Tennessee, exposed a web of police corruption of nationwide proportions. Police officials from every section of the country were found to be involved with some of the nation's most notorious criminals. As a result of public concern over police misconduct and governmental action to combat it, O. W. Wilson's consulting activities increased. City after city invited him to study their police agencies and to make recommendations for reform. He began to meticulously schedule his summer vacation time so that he could handle as many consulting jobs as possible.[11] Wilson's personal records reflect that from 1950 to 1960 he conducted management surveys of thirty-two major police agencies.

In the wake of wholesale indictments of Internal Revenue Service personnel, Wilson, John Holstrom, and Bruce Smith were commissioned by the Treasury Department to devise an internal inspections plan for the Alcohol, Tobacco, and Tax Unit, the Secret Service, the Internal Revenue Service, and Coast Guard Intelligence. The purpose of the plan was to implement a system of on-going inspections designed to ensure that the Treasury Department's investigative units maintained institutional integrity while functioning according to the principles of sound management. The study took one year to complete. Wilson made some ten trips to Washington. Each trip had two Wilsonian requirements: collect enough material to keep him busy for six weeks, and bring Patricia a present from Washington. Upon completing the study, Wilson and his colleagues submitted to the Treasury Department a manual of inspectional procedures, much of which is still in use.[12]

O. W. received a great deal of satisfaction from the Treasury Department survey, but his first love was municipal police administration. It was the surveys of city police departments which gave him his greatest satisfaction, for O. W. believed that he was making a substantial contribution to police professionalization in this way. The systematic manner in which he approached such ventures reflected this belief. Herman Goldstein, a former assistant to the city manager in Portland, Oregon, remembers the eight weeks which Wilson spent studying the Portland Police Department during the summer of 1954.

Goldstein had been appointed by his city manager to assist Wilson, who was working for the Public Administration Service. Portland was not a corrupt department, but it was a badly organized one, with poor morale, personnel problems, and a reputation for inefficiency and slovenliness.

Goldstein found O. W. Wilson to be thorough and precise. Before coming to Portland, O. W. sent city officials a questionnaire which asked for extensive background information on the department and the city. He also asked for copies of the budget, organization charts, training material, strength reports, and legal documents. Wilson did this so he could commence work immediately on arriving in the community. Once there, O. W. plunged into work, beginning early in the morning, laboring into the night. Goldstein was impressed by his meticulous attention to detail, and the comprehensive nature of his inquiry. Every facet of the department's operation was studied. The end product was a lengthy report which completely restructured the agency. In it, O. W.'s experiences in Wichita and in the army were apparent. Spans of control were reduced to workable numbers, command-control relationships were explicitly detailed, a rather rigid chain of command was established, strict personnel practices were recommended, an in-service training program was installed, and an internal inspectional procedure was created. In short, the police department was "whipped into shape."[13]

A close bond developed between O. W. Wilson and Herman Goldstein. Goldstein discovered that Wilson was almost completely preoccupied with police administration. Even during off-duty hours when the two relaxed over dinner or a drink, O. W. would spend much of the time mulling over possible solutions to the myriad of problems facing law enforcement in its struggle to professionalize. On his personal relationship with O. W., Goldstein stated that he:

> got as close as one could get to O. W., who had a degree of reservation, an aloofness. He built his bond with people based on a professional relationship. He did not have time to cultivate strong bonds outside the professional arena. He often gave the outward impression of coldness, but he was a very warm man to his few close friends.[14]

Wilson saw in Goldstein a bright, energetic young man who was capable of eventually making a considerable contribution to police administration. When O. W. Wilson was selected by the American Bar Association as the police advisor to their groundbreaking study of the American criminal justice system, he brought in Herman Goldstein to assist him, along with Roy C. McLaren, a former student who himself would someday become a distinguished police administrator.

Although O. W. Wilson had an obvious impact on law enforcement through his publications, his surveys, his administrative achievements, and through the accomplishments of his former students and subordinates, much of his influence has not been documented. For example, Wilson had a good deal of respect for the administrative ability of Los Angeles Police Chief William H. Parker. Nevertheless, Wilson felt that Parker did not always utilize fully the considerable resources at his disposal.[15] The Los Angeles Police Department had in its employ a psychiatrist, Dr. John Rankin. Yet the department was not using Dr. Rankin very extensively in either entrance examinations or in internal psychological evaluations or counseling. O. W., at a police conference in Los Angeles in 1952, brought Parker and the School of Criminology's psychiatrist, Dr. Douglas Kelley together. Wilson and Kelley convinced Chief Parker that Dr. Rankin's role in departmental affairs should be expanded. As a result, William H. Parker installed in the Los Angeles Police Department a system of psychological testing and evaluation which won the agency a reputation for leadership in the field. Kelley also played a part in another Wilsonian achievement.

In 1956, the Police Officers' Research Association of California (PORAC) met at its annual convention in San Diego. One of the first orders of business was to promulgate a law enforcement code of ethics. A committee was formed to develop such a code. It consisted of O. W. Wilson as chairman and Douglas Kelley, John Holstrom, and FBI Agent William Whelan. The committee struggled with the code, but found that its final draft was much too wordy. Holstrom asked Douglas Kelley to rewrite it into a brief one-page document. Kelley did, and PORAC adopted it.[16] The Law Enforcement Code of Ethics was later accepted by the International Association of Chiefs of Police (IACP), and by the entire police community. Credit for the Code was given to PORAC. However, even though historians have not traced the origins of the Code beyond the PORAC conference, Wilson's Square Deal Code in Wichita was its antecedent, as evidenced by the following exchange between Wilson and Holstrom during the course of an interview:

> *Wilson:* . . . The inception of the Code of Ethics came in Wichita and was outlined in the Square Deal Code. We adopted it there in the very early 30's. If you read that code you will find that much of it is incorporated in this Code of Ethics that has been accepted by the IACP. *Holstrom:* I now remember the Square Deal Code and I had forgotten it. Of course you developed it.[17]

So, O. W. Wilson was the father of law enforcement's Code of Ethics, not the PORAC committee of which he was a member.

In 1957, Dean Wilson accepted a long-standing offer to teach a summer course at the University of Hawaii. Between his teaching, his consulting activities and the time he had devoted to publishing journal articles, O. W. had not enjoyed a vacation in some time. Wilson believed that he owed it to Ruth and Patricia to take them on an extended vacation, albeit a working one. The Wilsons spent the entire summer in Honolulu, relaxing, visiting with friends such as Chief of Police Daniel Liu, and sightseeing. Wilson's light teaching load permitted him to spend considerable time with his family. O. W. was not particularly comfortable in Hawaii. He insisted on wearing the heavy dark suits and starched shirts which he had become accustomed to in the cooler climate of northern California. Yet, although he was quite uncomfortable in the tropical heat, Wilson refused to accept his wife's advice to dress more appropriately. He was Dean Orlando W. Wilson, America's foremost police administrator, and he would dress the part, despite the heat. Mrs. Wilson and Patricia, unlike O. W., enjoyed their Hawaiian vacation immensely. As the family returned to Berkeley at summer's end, Ruth Wilson committed herself to some day enticing Orlando into retiring in Hawaii.

During the academic year 1957-58, Dean Wilson received permission to appoint a criminology advisory committee. The committee, termed "The Mob," by Wilson, was composed of police and corrections officials. The mission of "The Mob" was to provide the School of Criminology with input on changes in the academic program.[18] The group was later to play a more important role in the affairs of criminology.

Dean Wilson's School of Criminology flourished. It received the full support of President Sproul, who sheltered it from the political machinations which were characteristic of the Berkeley campus.[19] When Sproul decided to retire, however, he was replaced by Clark Kerr, a man who neither sympathized nor identified with the program, its faculty, or its objectives. This change in administration was to mean a perceptible change in the support Wilson and his school would receive from the university.

When Kerr ascended to the presidency, John Holstrom was sure that he would attempt to destroy the School of Criminology. Kerr had for years been chancellor of the Berkeley campus, but had been restrained from embarking on a collision course with Criminology due to Sproul's support of the school. Holstrom, as Berkeley Chief of Police, had experienced several confrontations with Clark Kerr which led him to believe that Kerr had an aversion to force and violence. Since he viewed policemen as forceful, violent people, and since a considerable number of criminology students were either policemen or police hopefuls, Holstrom felt trouble was imminent.

Shortly after Clark Kerr had been appointed Chancellor of the University of California at Berkeley, Chief Holstrom paid a courtesy call on him. Chancellor Kerr, right after Holstrom introduced himself, launched into a tirade against the Berkeley Police Department's harassment of students. He accused Holstrom of keeping dossiers on students and faculty, and would not listen to the chief's explanation. Holstrom found Kerr quite belligerent. On another occasion, Chief Holstrom and his city manager were summoned to the Chancellor's office following a panty raid involving several thousand students. Kerr, face flushed and voice trembling, demanded to know why the Berkeley Police had allowed the incident to take place. Holstrom explained that there had been no injuries, but Chancellor Kerr was in no mood for excuses. Tempers flared between Kerr and Holstrom, and the Chief stalked from the meeting.[20]

Clark Kerr also had a reputation as an "academic elitist." That is, he believed that the primary role of the university's undergraduate programs was to produce graduate students who would be molded into scholars. Thus, professional education, outside the Schools of Law and Medicine, was viewed with disdain by Kerr, who felt that it was the job of the state colleges. Rumors reached Wilson that the president was displeased over the absence of doctoral degrees on its faculty. When it was suggested that even the Dean should enroll in a doctoral program, Wilson remarked rather haughtily, "And who is there to teach *me?*"[21]

A warning of things to come occurred in the spring of 1957 when, at the behest of Kerr, the Academic Advisory Committee conducted an investigation of the School of Criminology. After some study, the Committee recommended that the School be prohibited from embarking on any program of expansion, and that it reduce the number of professional courses in its curriculum. In a memorandum, Wilson responded that:

> Since law enforcement and corrections agencies are making every effort to professionalize their services, we believe it would be highly inconsistent for us to be required to reduce the number of professional courses offered to students in these fields.[22]

Kerr assigned the Committee on Educational Policy to fully review the school's curriculum, and to make recommendations on its future role in university affairs. The committee forwarded to Dean Wilson a comprehensive questionnaire designed to elicit from Wilson his perspective on the objectives of his program. After a six-month investigation, the Committee on Educational Policy refused to give a definitive recommendation concerning the school's future. It strongly suggested to President Kerr that he appoint a special group to study the School of Criminology. Kerr accepted the recommendation. He informed Wilson that, pending action by the committee, there would be a moratorium on new courses in and tenured appointments to the school. A special *ad hoc* committee, under the chairmanship of Professor James M. Cline, was appointed to investigate Criminology.[23] In the summer of 1959, the committee reported back to President Kerr.

The Cline Committee recommended "discontinuance of the School," and proposed that "this type of training be developed and implemented in the state colleges." It contended that "the undergraduate program is not suitable for a university," and "the faculty of the School is not qualified by personality or scholarship to carry out a graduate program."[24]

O. W. Wilson was livid. He at first decided to immediately resign in protest over the report; however, Austin MacCormick talked him out of it. Both Wilson and MacCormick viewed Clark Kerr as a weak man, one who would buckle to outside pressure. After conferring with the Criminology faculty, Wilson moved to exert that pressure. Dean Wilson and MacCormick went to "The Mob" for assistance. They prepared a detailed fifty-one page report attacking the Cline Committee findings, and chronicling the accomplishments of the school. The criminal justice community responded to Wilson's plea for aid by launching a major lobbying campaign to persuade university officials not to discontinue Criminology.[25]

The effort to save the School of Criminology was spearheaded by the California Director of Corrections, Richard McGee, a political force in the state. He chaired a luncheon meeting of criminal justice administrators and members of the Cline Committee, at which the justice community's support of the school was made clear to university officials. Joining in the effort to save the school were the governor, the state attorney general, district attorneys, sheriffs, police chiefs, corrections executives, and state legislators. In the face of such strength, Clark Kerr backed away from his plans to discontinue the criminology curriculum. He appointed a committee to review the findings of the Cline Committee. This group, referred to rather derisively by the criminology faculty as "the committee on the committee," would later vote to continue the school, with some curriculum revision.[26]

O. W. Wilson was fatigued following his more than two year fight to save the School of Criminology. He was almost sixty years old, and he was beginning to feel his age. Ruth Wilson took the opportunity to press her husband for another trip to Hawaii. Dean Wilson was entitled to a one-year sabbatical leave. After some urging, O. W. reluctantly agreed to take it in Hawaii, where he would revise *Police Administration* and reflect on the direction which criminology should travel in the future.

Wilson's request for a sabbatical leave was approved by the university, and Ruth excitedly made their travel plans. Police Chief Dan Liu was contacted in Honolulu and asked to help in their relocation. In a gesture of affection for Ruth, Wilson purchased a new wardrobe, one which was appropriate to tropical weather.[27]

Orlando W. Wilson would never wear his new wardrobe. Events were occurring which would lead to a cancellation of his trip and propel him toward the police superintendency in Chicago. At sixty years of age, Wilson would take on his greatest challenge.

8

A PURITAN IN BABYLON

When in 1928 a Cook County grand jury characterized the Chicago Police Department as "rotten to the core,"[1] it was articulating a recurring theme in the history of that troubled agency. Ten years later, following a survey of the department, noted police authority Bruce Smith charged that the agency was so corrupt, the mayor should fire and replace every single officer. Intermittent police scandals in Chicago had, over the years, eroded citizens' confidence in police officers. Exposés of graft and corruption were frequent and widespread. On those few occasions when public clamor for improvement led to police reform, that reform was superficial and ephemeral.[2] Political expedience was not usually compatible with police reform, so long-term reformation often fell by the wayside when citizen concern abated.

In Chicago, the dominant political mode has been termed "the Irish style." The Irish conception of politics was that office holders had an obligation to employ needy relatives and able-bodied Irishmen in government jobs, as policemen, firefighters, and blue collar workers. Frequently, Chicago police officers viewed their positions as a source of graft. At first distinctions were often made between "honest graft" and "dishonest graft," with the former being a payoff for permitting socially acceptable vice to flourish, while the latter represented remuneration for allowing socially unacceptable activity, such as narcotics traffic, to continue.[3] Unfortunately, in time, the distinction between "honest" and "dishonest" graft blurred in Chicago. As a result, police corruption was commonplace activity. Even honest mayors found it politically suicidal to crack down on corruption, for it would have meant the dismissal or indictment of thousands of policemen: sons of the voting public.

Thus, corruption continued under the watchful eye of political bosses, many of whom participated, but some of whom did not.[4] In 1960, however, a police scandal occurred which made reform not only politically feasible, but essential.

In early January 1960, a young thief named Richard Morrison was arrested for burglary in Chicago. He subsequently confessed to the offense, implicating eight Chicago policemen assigned to the Summerdale District Station. Four large vans were used to move contraband from the officers' homes.[5] It was immediately termed by the press as "the Summerdale Scandal," and it caused a public furor. Mayor Richard J. Daley, who had been vacationing in Key West, came home to a crisis. Upon arrival in Chicago, he met in conference with top advisors to plan strategy which would blunt the criticism of his administration.[6]

Mayor Daley decided that he would have to take bold steps in order to mute criticism of his administration and undertake police reform. It was now politically feasible to clean up the department, and he moved to do just that. Daley's detractors have questioned his sincerity in reforming the Chicago Police Department. One knowledgeable observer holds, however, that Mayor Daley sincerely desired police reform, for he loved his city and believed that continued police corruption besmirched its image. In any event, Daley decided to appoint a five-member search committee to recommend a reform police commissioner. The members would be Franklin Kreml,[7] Director of Northwestern University's renowned Traffic Institute, one of the most distinguished figures in American law enforcement; Paul Goodrich, President of the Chicago Association of Commerce and Industry; Virgil Peterson, Director of the Chicago Crime Commission; William F. McFetridge, International President of the Building Service Employees Union; and O. W. Wilson, who would chair the committee.[8]

Wilson had been recommended by the mayor's press aide Earl Bush, who had once read Wilson's *Police Administration.* Mike Royko has alleged that Daley selected O. W. as his new commissioner before he was invited to serve on the committee, yet the mayor did not directly offer him the post because it would smack of a political appointment. So, according to Royko, Wilson was invited to Chicago as chairman of the search committee, where he would eventually be enticed into accepting the commissionership, thereby heading off allegations that the mayor had orchestrated the appointment. Royko was not able to support this theory with evidence, and Franklin Kreml holds that the premise has no basis in fact.[9]

Timothy O'Connor, the incumbent commissioner, was ordered by Mayor Daley to resign. He submitted his resignation on 18 January 1960, but it was not made public until 24 January. On that day, the mayor announced O'Connor's resignation and the appointment of the search committee.[10] Wilson flew to Chicago to chair the committee and participate in its deliberations.

Mayor Daley charged the committee with "picking the best man that can be found anywhere in the nation." The committee was also assigned to recommend policies designed to upgrade the police department. The search committee decided to conduct its deliberations in a private conference room at the University Club. At their first meeting, they established general criteria to guide them in the selection process. The man who would eventually be selected commissioner would have to demonstrate integrity, professional skill, and high-level administrative experience. A primary requisite was incorruptibility. The International Association of Chiefs of Police was invited to recommend candidates.[11]

The committee met for twenty-eight days, amidst speculation by the news media over who would be the new commissioner. Meetings often lasted from early morning to late night. It was not unusual for members to eat both lunch and dinner at the conference table. Mercifully, committee members developed a congenial relationship which allowed them to perform their task with a minimum of friction. The long hours and hard work were so severe that one member, Bill McFetridge, became ill, and was advised by his physician to withdraw from membership. He refused.[12]

The preliminary business of the committee was to evaluate the more than one hundred résumés which had been submitted for evaluation. Many applicants were clearly unqualified, so that they were summarily eliminated from consideration. Those applicants who were identified as prime candidates were invited to Chicago for an interview. Any Chicago policemen who applied, and there were a number who did, were personally interviewed by the committee, regardless of their rank or assignment. Committee members felt that they owed this extra consideration to the department, and in extending it might "strike gold" in the ranks. They did not.

The work was quite frustrating. Many of the résumés which had been submitted for the committee's evaluation were considerably more impressive than the actual candidates. Those few men who had been identified as prime candidates were interviewed for a least one hour, and usually longer. Wilson moderated the questioning. His manner was crisp and businesslike, but not brusque. The interrogation was designed to uncover the subject's attitude, values, and judgment. Committee members questioned all interviewees in the same order. First came Goodrich, then McFetridge, Peterson, Kreml, and Wilson. O. W.'s questions covered the technical aspects of police administration, and they were usually situational. The Dean, as he was called by McFetridge, tried to elicit from candidates answers to hypothetical administrative problems. Following each interview, the candidate would be excused, whereupon the committee would discuss him. The result was a meeting of the minds on whether the candidate should be eliminated from further consideration, or if he should be listed among the finalists. Mayor Richard Daley took no part in the deliberations.[13]

The committee was not particularly pleased with the general quality of the applicants. Since some rather well-known police administrators had applied for the commissionership, it may have been an indictment of the state of American law enforcement that few seemed to measure up to even the most fundamental qualifications. Nevertheless, by Saturday, 20 February, the committee had narrowed its focus to five finalists. Each member was asked to rate the five according to preference. The ratings seemed to match up well, as a top candidate was selected.[14] Then, one member asked, "Can we go to the mayor with this guy and really say he has all we need?" After a brief silence, the answer was clear: the best law enforcement had offered was not good enough to fill the Chicago commissionership and do the job which needed to be done. At that point, Bill McFetridge suggested that the appropriate candidate was a member of the committee, in the person of either Franklin Kreml or O. W. Wilson.[15]

Kreml forcefully withdrew himself from consideration. Although his law enforcement qualifications were impeccable, Kreml was not willing to abandon his contractual obligation to Northwestern University. Next, attention shifted to Wilson, who initially declined consideration. However, with the four members of the committee hammering away at him, especially the forceful and persuasive Kreml and McFetridge, O. W. agreed to "sit in the end chair" and be interviewed the following day, though he warned the committee that the prospect of his taking the job was slight.

The next morning, Sunday, O. W. Wilson sat in the end chair, answering many of the questions he had posed to other candidates. He took the interrogation seriously, but with some forebearance; he was not overwhelmed by the experience. Still, his performance was impressive—so much so that the committee was soon convinced that Wilson was their only real candidate. For a full hour following the questioning, the committee tried to talk him into accepting their nomination. He declined. The job was too political, and since he had committed himself to a sabbatical, it would be unfair to Ruth and Patricia.[16] O. W. remained rigid in his refusal until the committee called on his sense of duty.

It was pointed out that in a very real way his entire career had been pointed to this challenge, and that he had an obligation to use his expertise to cure the malaise which gripped the Chicago Police Department. Reluctantly, Wilson agreed to accept the post—but only if certain conditions were met. He wanted a three-year contract at $30,000 a year, more than twice as much as he was presently making, and $7,500 dollars more than the last commissioner's salary. He also demanded independence from political pressure and the creation of a police board, consisting of the surviving members of the search committee, to oversee the police department and to insulate him from politics. A final requirement was a guarantee that his $30,000 salary would be paid, regardless of what happened to him. Municipal law prohibited the city from financially committing itself to an employment contract beyond one year, so the second- and third-year salary would have to be insured in case the city decided not to honor the agreement. Committee members Peterson, Goodrich, and McFetridge pledged the ten thousand dollars necessary to insure the contract with Lloyd's of London. Franklin Kreml would make the arrangements. The committee agreed to recommend to Mayor Daley that he meet Wilson's other demands. The mayor was called at home and told that the committee had selected a new commissioner. He immediately came to the University Club.[17]

On Sunday afternoon, Mayor Daley met with the search committee, in the same conference room that had been the site of its deliberations. He was told of the committee's choice of O. W. Wilson, and Wilson's requirements. He approved, but decided that it would be prudent to check with the corporation counsel, John C. Melaniphy, who was summoned to the scene. When Melaniphy arrived, he stunned the group by pointing out that, since the commissioner is a governmental officership, as defined in the Illinois Constitution, it must be filled by a state resident. Mayor Daley was visibly disturbed. He asked the corporation counsel if there was a way in which Wilson could assume the post and still be consistent with law. Melaniphy suggested that a local ordinance could be drafted which would give the proposed police board all the powers of the commissionership. Wilson would then serve under the board, as its executive officer. In fact, O. W. would really administer the agency; the plan would simply be a device to sidestep the residence requirement, although it would be necessary to change the term "commissioner" to "superintendent." Mayor Daley ordered his corporation counsel to draw up the ordinance by the following day. Melaniphy did, and Daley was convinced that it would withstand any court test.[18]

On Monday afternoon, 22 February, Mayor Richard Daley called a press conference in his office, at which he announced the selection committee's choice of O. W. Wilson. He said that he would submit Wilson's name to the City Council for approval on 2 March, along with the new ordinance prepared by Corporation Counsel Melaniphy.[19] He summarized Wilson's requirements for taking the job, described the proposed ordinance, discussed the police board concept, then closed with a pledge that "there will be no (political) influence of any kind from any source." O. W. made it clear that he would expose any attempt at political interference to the press, then resign.[20]

Reaction to Wilson's appointment was mixed. When the *Chicago Tribune* conducted a survey of Chicago policemen, it found that in most cases, the reaction reflected the officers' age and rank. Veteran officers were generally bitter over the appointment, the younger men seemed delighted, and high-ranking officers were either critical or noncommital. A police captain termed it "the worst thing that ever happened to the department." A jailor said, "It doesn't affect me. Nothing does." A veteran detective said, "If this had come when I was in my prime I'd be a captain today. Now? Who cares?" A young patrolman stated, "I'm delighted. I hope he gets a free hand."[21]

Wilson flew back to Berkeley to prepare for his move to Chicago. He had one week to do so. Ruth and Patricia, although disappointed over cancellation of the Hawaiian trip, nonetheless were thrilled over O. W.'s appointment. They would remain in Berkeley until the summer because of Patricia's school attendance.[22] Just before Wilson went back to Chicago, he set out to attend to one last piece of business.

Organized crime had become deeply entrenched in Chicago. Wilson knew that in order to successfully battle the mob, he would need the cooperation of the Federal government, especially the FBI. Because O. W. and J. Edgar Hoover were involved in a long-standing feud, Wilson decided to make an overture to Director Hoover. He contacted a special agent assigned to the San Francisco office whom he had known for a long time. He told the agent to ask Hoover what it would take "to bury the hatchet." The following day, the agent reported back to O. W.: "Forget it." The director was not willing to "bury the hatchet."[23] Wilson left for Chicago knowing that he could expect no assistance from J. Edgar Hoover.[24]

Wilson's appointment to the superintendency was approved on 2 March, and he went to work immediately. He took up temporary residence at the centrally located University Club.[25] Wilson approached the challenge with a clearcut idea of his role and the job which needed to be done. He was an executive, a top administrator. He would sit at the top of the police department's organizational structure, planning, directing, controlling, issuing policy, delegating authority and responsibility, organizing and deploying resources. He was not a line policeman, he was an executive; so he had no need for a uniform or a gun. Wilson would never wear a uniform, carry a firearm, or drive a car. He had a chauffeur-driven limousine placed at his disposal.

Superintendent Wilson's first official act was to select a staff. He had decided that although it would be necessary to bring in personnel from outside the department, he would not attempt to bestow on them police rank. Instead, they would be given civilian titles, such as "director" or "assistant to," in order to forestall possible morale problems among the rank and file. The superintendent went after men who had served him well in the past. An International Association of Chiefs of Police management survey team, led by former Wichita lieutenant Ray Ashworth, had been brought to Chicago to conduct a reorganization study, so that Wilson had the services of several consultants whom he knew and respected. The IACP consultative staff was to work closely with him, especially during his first year in office.[26] In terms of a permanent staff, O. W. moved quickly to surround himself with trusted aides.

The first man he contacted was Minor Keith Wilson, who had worked for O. W. in the army. Keith Wilson had recently retired a full colonel, and was in Washington, D. C, enrolled in graduate school taking courses in public administration. On his first day in office, the superintendent called Keith and tersely said, "I'd like you to join me." Keith asked if it could wait until the end of the semester, whereupon O. W. replied, "No, I want you now." As Keith was mulling the offer over, his wife grasped the receiver from him and said, "O. W. he'll be with you day after tomorrow." Keith joined his friend on 4 March. He was appointed aide to O. W. and legal advisor.

Wilson secured Herman Goldstein as his executive assistant. Goldstein had been with Wilson during the survey of the Portland Police Department and in the American Bar Foundation study. Dick McDonnel had been a graduate student of Wilson's at Berkeley, as had George O'Connor. Both were bright young men whom O. W. had identified as potentially fine professionals years before. McDonnel was brought in as a planner, O'Connor directed the Training Division. Wilson enticed Jacques Boyer away from the state of Pennsylvania and hired him as director of personnel.[27]

This was the core of his staff, along with part-time consultants and high-ranking police administrators. They worked well together. Their individual styles ranged from scholarly to pragmatic, and their personalities ran the gamut from gregarious to reserved. But they all had three things in common: each was fiercely loyal to O. W.; each had a burning desire to help him succeed; all were selfless, content to bask in the reflected glory of their superintendent. O. W. used his staff well.

His door was always open to them. He listened to them and often implemented their suggestions. Their collective brainstorming, which was encouraged by Wilson, often led to fruitful projects. One of their most important contributions, however, was made during the early days of O. W.'s superintendency. They were a source of loyalty and devotion on which Wilson could rely at a time when police personnel were largely unknown quantities.

The task that Superintendent Wilson and his staff faced in rebuilding the Chicago Police Department was monumental. To the precise, systematic, orderly O. W. Wilson, the organizational structure was a nightmare, politics played much too large a role in departmental affairs, up-to-date equipment was lacking, there was an absence of effective leadership, corruption was widespread, and even the most fundamental tenets of contemporary police administration were not in evidence. Corruption in the Chicago Police Department was everywhere; it had become institutionalized over the years until it was expected behavior among officers, though not everyone was corrupt. A number of officers had remained untarnished, even among the higher ranks. Nevertheless, it appeared that the dominant characteristic of Chicago law enforcement was corruption.

Morale was low. The Summerdale Scandal, coupled with public reaction to it, had helped create an atmosphere of anxiety among policemen. The replacement of a popular Irish Catholic police commissioner who had risen to the commissionership through the ranks with an outsider who was neither Irish nor Catholic added to the rank and file's anxiety.[28]

The police department's physical facilities were run-down and ill-equipped. The previous commissioner had attempted to ingratiate himself with the city administration by keeping his budgets as low as possible and by returning vast amounts of unexpended funds at the end of each fiscal year. The results of this continuing austerity program were dingy, badly furnished district stations; a dirty, run-down police headquarters; too few, overused patrol cars; cramped facilities; and a shortage of even the most basic equipment. The absence of file cabinets at police headquarters meant that records had to be stored in cardboard boxes. Policemen had to bring their own typewriters to work or purchase used ones. Desk sergeants paid for carbon paper out of their own pockets. Because of a shortage of desks and chairs, policemen in the district stations would either construct needed furniture out of used lumber, or "borrow" it from cooperative merchants. There appeared to be no system of command responsibility for the actions of subordinates. In-service training was almost nonexistent. Two radio frequencies were all that served the police force of this city of more than three million residents. It was not unusual for a citizen to experience a three-hour wait for a patrol car to respond to a call for service.[29] Supervision of the patrol force was inadequate, largely because no sergeancy promotions had been made for years. The supervisory selection process had become so corrupt that it was common knowledge that a patrolman could ensure his advancement with a $700 bribe, a sum described by a reporter "as rigid as if it had been fixed by the Federal Reserve Board." This distrust of the promotional system had led to a series of lawsuits and injunctions by disgruntled police officers. Consequently, the entire process was such a subject of litigation that the Civil Service Commission had simply stopped making promotions in order to avoid controversy.[30]

Political interference in the daily operations of the police department took many forms, but it was at the district level where the intrusion of partisan politics was most apparent. Chicago had thirty-eight district police stations, each of which was commanded by a captain. The police department generally, and the district stations in particular, were parts of the Democratic political machine. The department was a source of patronage jobs, while aldermen and ward committeemen controlled law enforcement in their districts. In effect, each alderman functioned as the mayor of a community, with the district captain acting as his chief of police. Aldermen would choose their own captains and control promotions, assignments, and transfers of personnel. Crime control existed to the extent that a district alderman permitted it. Mayor Daley presided over this system. The police commissioner's office was located in City Hall, right next to the mayor's.[31]

Superintendent Wilson did not delude himself into believing that Mayor Daley intended to completely relinquish his control over police operations. But Wilson was hopeful that the mayor would discontinue his interference in day-to-day police administration. Daley's influence on police management would come by way of the newly organized Police Board, to which the mayor appointed three holdovers from the search committee: Franklin Kreml, Bill McFetridge, and Paul Goodrich, along with two newcomers, Morgan F. Murphy, Vice-President of Commonwealth Edison, and Theophilus Mann, a black attorney. Specifically, the board had four major functions: to review and approve police budgets, to establish departmental rules and regulations, to act as an appellate authority in disciplinary actions, and to recommend to the mayor nominees for future superintendencies. Kreml was president of the board. Kreml was viewed by Wilson as a friend, but more important, he was a professional who could be counted on to support the superintendent's programs, if Wilson could justify them. Goodrich and Mann were believed to be relatively neutral. Murphy and McFetridge were personally close to the mayor. It was through them, Wilson was convinced, that Daley's influence would be felt. O. W. was not precisely sure what shape it would take, but he thought that it would probably come in the form of resistance to his budgets. Superintendent Wilson felt, however, that despite the fact that McFetridge and Murphy were agents of the mayor, they were both honorable, reasonable men who could generally be counted on for support in his reform efforts.[32]

At the onset of his tenure, Wilson's immediate future was clouded by the possibility that his appointment and the creation of the Police Board were illegal. In order to formalize the action taken by the City Council, a statute had to be enacted by the state legislature. No one was sure how the legislature would react ot the proposed statute. Furthermore, Cook County state's attorney Benjamin Adamowski, a Republican rival of Mayor Daley, initiated a campaign to invalidate O. W. Wilson's selection. Adamowski charged that Wilson was ineligible to serve as head of the police department because of his lack of residency. He said that O. W.'s nomination had been "rigged" by the Police Board, which itself was illegally constituted. Adamowski stepped up his attack on Wilson by charging that he had been "brainwashed" into believing the mayor would allow him to reform the Chicago Police Department. When the charge was denied by Wilson, Adamowski branded the superintendent's response "as patent a lie as anyone can speak." The state's attorney then filed a motion with the state supreme court asking it to set aside the Wilson appointment and void the Police Board.[33] Throughout the controversy, O. W. stood aloof. Eventually, state legislation was passed finalizing his superintendency and the creation of the board, and state's attorney Adamowski's suit was dismissed.[34]

O. W. could not help but follow closely the legal controversies surrounding his appointment; however, no useful purpose would have been served by permitting them to distract him from the work for which he had been hired. So, in typical Wilsonian fashion, he publicly ignored the dispute, while focusing on the job at hand. His first few weeks in office were a whirlwind of activity. He initially concentrated on two high priority items: to free the Chicago Police Department of corruption and to reorganize the department.[35]

Since the department's more than ten thousand personnel were unknown to him and the civilian staff he had brought in was relatively small, it was necessary to identify policemen who could immediately assume more responsible duties. Wilson contracted with a management consultant firm to interview command officers and draft a three- or four-page psychological profile of each man. The profile summarized each subject's motivation, judgment, and qualities of leadership. These profiles turned out to be rather accurate, in most cases.[36] From personal contact with officers, their past record, and the information on the psychological profiles, O. W. Wilson selected his command staff.

Wilson arranged his department in pyramidal form. Immediately beneath him in the chain of command Wilson created three bureaus: the Bureau of Staff Services, the Bureau of Field Services, and the Bureau of Inspectional Services, commanded respectively by Pierce Fleming, James B. Conlisk, Jr., and Joseph F. Morris. All had been handpicked by the superintendent. To make room at the top for his new appointments, O. W. swept less qualified men aside with disdain, almost as if inefficiency was a form of corruption. He reduced Kyran Phelan, who had been acting commissioner prior to Wilson, to the rank of captain. Two retired police officers serving as aides to the commissioner were fired to make room for Herman Goldstein and Keith Wilson. He demoted the chief of the uniformed force and his deputy chief, and the deputy superintendent of field services. Several district commanders were transferred. Throughout his superintendency, Wilson was to exhibit a ruthlessness in personnel transfers and discipline which had previously been unknown in Chicago.[37] Although he may not have taken pleasure from invoking disciplinary action, it is clear that such duties were not painful.

Of the three deputy superintendents, the most sensitive assignment was given to Joe Morris, as commander of the Bureau of Inspectional Services. Wilson grew to admire the veteran officer. Morris had the reputation of incorruptibility, which may have been the reason why an anti-hoodlum squad he formed some years before had been abandoned. He was tough, fearless, intelligent, resourceful, and street-wise. He knew the police department intimately, and he did not particularly like what he saw. Wilson placed four specialized units in Morris's Bureau: the Internal Investigation Division (IID), the Intelligence Division, the Inspection Division, and the Vice Division. The division commanders, like Morris, held ranks which were exempt from civil service protection, thereby giving Wilson firm control over them. They were termed "directors," and wore the insignia of army majors. The Internal Investigation Division was ordered to conduct vigorous investigations of suspected misconduct among officers, while the Inspection Division had as its assignment the continuing inspection of the department and its physical facilities so that recommendations for improvement could be made.[38] Neither function had ever been undertaken on the Chicago Police Department.

The IID set out to fulfill a mandate issued by Superintendent Wilson: end corruption. The tactics of this division were to earn O. W. the lasting enmity of many members of the rank and file. Complaints from citizens were solicited by the division. Armed with information from the community, IID investigators moved against officers suspected of corruption. Investigators posed as traffic violators on Lakeshore Drive to see if patrolmen solicited bribes during encounters with drivers. They acted as skid row drunks to determine if beat police officers rifled their pockets for valuables. They infiltrated the jail to check on booking procedures, prisoner treatment, and jailer honesty. Chicago policemen found abusing their positions were fired and indicted. When there was a doubt over the guilt or innocence of a policeman, the suspected officer was ordered to take a polygraph examination. If he refused to take one, or if he failed the test, he was summarily dismissed. IID continued its aggressive campaign amidst criticism from the rank and file over its methods and allegations that it was illegally entrapping officers into violating the law.

In an attempt to win personnel over to the idea of police reform, the superintendent assembled five thousand patrolmen for a face-to-face meeting in the International Amphitheatre. He told them of his philosophy, his plans for more and better equipment, his resolve to rid the department of corruption, and his continuing commitment to police professionalization.[39] His talk was cheered, but there were also other reactions, including comments and outbursts by individual officers which were openly disrespectful. O. W. neither understood nor approved of this conduct. He was the superintendent, and although he never required the love or affection of his men, he felt that he was entitled to their respect. Some officers never gave it. Even on those occasions when Wilson was invited to police social functions, such as banquets or picnics, he was often the target of derisive comments, snide remarks, and open hostility. There is some evidence to suggest that he limited his contact with the rank and file in order to avoid their verbal abuse.[40]

Following his meeting with patrolmen, Superintendent Wilson ordered high-ranking officers to meet with him. At a closed meeting of sixty-eight supervisors and commanders, Wilson demanded their loyalty, told them to invoke disciplinary action against errant policemen, and promised to protect them from political influence. He vowed to report to the press any political interference, and called on them to end the "Chicago Tradition," in which policemen gave preferential treatment to other policemen involved in criminal law violations. The superintendent was well received.[41]

O. W. Wilson's aggressive anticorruption campaign generally pleased the community and the news media, but it produced opposition internally. Frank Carey, President of the Patrolman's Association[42] and the department's Catholic chaplain, Father Patrick McPolin, both spoke out against the superintendent. Frank Carey was a blunt, coarse, tough-talking career patrolman who was convinced that the Chicago Police Department was being ruined by Wilson, whom Carey felt was an ivory-towered puritan. Carey had enjoyed a special relationship with the previous commissioner, who permitted the president to devote his entire working day to association business. O. W. discontinued the practice. He informed Frank, in a friendly way, that as long as he was on the payroll of the Chicago Police Department, he would do police work.[43]

Father McPolin had a yearly fund-raising event in which he used gambling equipment to generate revenue. Technically, it was a violation of the law, although it had been sanctioned by preceding administrations. Wilson ended the practice. The superintendent may also have alienated Father McPolin by adding a Protestant and Jewish chaplain to the department, which had historically been served exclusively by a Catholic priest. Both Carey and McPolin represented thorns in his side, sowing the seeds of discontent among the troops, openly criticizing him, trying to foster restiveness in the ranks. Carey became so disenchanted with O. W. Wilson that he embarked on an unsuccessful campaign to have Wilson fired.

When it became obvious to Frank Carey that the superintendent was unshakable in his resolve to reform the police department, Carey dispatched off-duty patrolmen to Berkeley and Wichita to conduct investigations into O. W.'s background. The purpose was to uncover embarrassing or damaging information about Wilson's personal life. The investigators met with no success, as more often than not they encountered people who respected and admired Wilson and had nothing but complimentary remarks to make. Carey tried to convince Chicago's newspapers that O. W. drank heavily, but they were not interested.[44]

As Superintendent Wilson saw that he would never convert Carey to his side, be began to use the patrolman as a foil. Carey's vulgar outbursts in the media were perfectly countered by the softspoken, scholarly superintendent. He sought to illustrate to Chicago's citizenry the contrast between the old and the new way, with Carey representing Summerdale, and Wilson reform. O. W. came off well in the contrast.

O. W. Wilson knew that he had a serious morale problem on his hands. IID's activities, although necessary, were contributing to rank and file anxiety. Wilson, in characteristic oversimplification, thought he could allay it by remodeling the department's buildings and by purchasing new furnishings and equipment. He completely remodeled police headquarters. Functional furnishings were purchased. Typewriters, file cabinets, and office machinery became plentiful. He did the same for district stations.[45]

Wilson moved his office from City Hall to the fourth floor of police headquarters. Some observers believed that the relocation was made by O. W. to symbolize the department's new-found independence from politics. Actually, the move was more pragmatic, as Wilson felt that it was impractical to be physically separated from the department.[46]

Wilson cultivated his relationship with the news media. He met with reporters often, and always tried to make himself available to them. Journalists, with few exceptions, liked him. They saw him as a sincere, dedicated professional; a positive force for needed police reform. Editorially, the four major newspapers supported him.[47] The *Chicago Daily News* serialized *Police Administration*, publishing it chapter by chapter. But, despite widespread media acceptance, his programs cost money, and it was only the politicians who could provide the funds necessary for Wilson to do his job. So, it was to them he would ultimately have to go for support.

A great deal of planning went into Wilson's initial budget. First year priorities had to be set, a difficult task because Wilson did not yet have a firm understanding of the department's operations. The priorities he set offered an interesting view of his professional values. Wilson's first budget was designed to lay the "superstructure" of a model department. As such, it was viewed as a first fiscal step in a continuing reform effort. The budget was eighty-four million dollars, an increase of approximately eleven million dollars over the previous year. The emphasis was on equipment: cars, furniture for district stations, communication gear, and records keeping equipment. O. W. admitted that it was a calculated risk, but added that "it was senseless to add more men while police communications, vehicles, and stations were out of date."[48] After his budget easily passed the Police Board, he spent three hours successfully defending it before the City Council. When the document was forwarded to the mayor, he approved it intact.

The Chicago Police Department's critical need for more supervisory officers brought Wilson into a collision course with the Civil Service Commission. The commission, which was very sensitive to political influence, moved very slowly, if at all, on controversial issues.[49] Because of the litigation that usually accompanied police promotional examinations, the Civil Service Commission simply avoided administering them, in spite of the superintendent's request for new sergeants. Despite the threat of lawsuits by the Patrolman's Association, and with the Civil Service Commission looking on in disbelief, Wilson made 125 patrolmen "temporary sergeants," and assigned them as squad leaders. Fifty of these "temporary sergeants" were black.

Wilson approached the Civil Service Commission once again to ask it to administer an examination. They agreed to do so. The superintendent, whose temporary promotions had bullied the commission into action, used his newly won influence to lessen the requirements of seniority, to dictate the type of examinations he wanted, and to loosen some of the traditional criteria which had characterized the police promotional process. The commission approved all of Wilson's ideas, and the system of promoting policemen in Chicago had at last been unclogged. With the relaxation of irrelevant requirements, talented men were able to move from patrolman to captain within five years, an unheard of occurrence prior to 1960.

Wilson seized the moment to infuse more blacks into ranks of policemen. O. W.'s staff conducted a study to determine why there were so few black police officers. The study revealed that although there was no shortage of black applicants, they were being weeded out in the selection process. Many were simply eliminated because of flat feet. When Wilson strongly suggested that the Civil Service Commission should reevaluate its prohibition against flat feet, it did away with the requirement altogether. By 1962, the Chicago Police Department had approximately 9,000 patrolmen, 1,200 of whom were black.[50] It represented a gain of some 500 black officers in two years.

Superintendent Wilson's daily work routine was formidable. A major part of each working day was devoted to planning and problem solving. It began early, often before eight in the morning, and continued into the early evening or beyond. A typical day might be devoted to a series of meetings with aides, a press conference, possibly a speech before a civic group, a short briefing of the mayor, and a tour of a district station. Lunch was always taken at the University Club, and was often a working meal. He would usually be accompanied by aides, who were in the midst of an important project.[51]

Concern consistently centered around the way in which departmental policy could reinforce the superintendent's pledge to end corruption. To simply forbid corruption was not enough for Wilson. He had to enact rigid rules which would discourage practices that contributed to misconduct. For example, he issued an order which he was confident could cut down traffic bribes. All officers were ordered to obey the following procedures when they stopped traffic violators: accept a driver's license only after it has been removed from the wallet by the violator, do not discuss cash bail or the amount of a fine, never sit in a violator's car, arrest immediately any violator who offers a bribe, and keep red flashing lights on throughout a traffic stop.[52] Once a policy was issued to officers, it was then released to the press. Wilson's policy formulation process was precise and systematic. Nevertheless, there was one occasion when it did not produce the intended result.

Ruth and Patricia Wilson were scheduled to move to Chicago in June, which meant that O. W. had to take time off from his busy schedule to find a home. He instructed an aide to pinpoint the residential area within the city limits which had the lowest crime rate. He then scoured the area for an appropriate house. When he found several possibilities, he photographed them, and sent the pictures to Ruth for evaluation. She responded by telling O. W. to buy any of the homes except one she had marked, which she described as "ghastly." Wilson then mistakenly bought the very house Ruth had asked him not to. It was too small to entertain in, and it could not accommodate all the Wilson furniture. When Mrs. Wilson saw the house, she scored O. W. for his inattention to detail.[53] It may have been the only time in his long career that Wilson had ever been accused of such slovenliness.

During Wilson's first year in office, the creation of an innovative records system, the beginning of a major communication network and the installation of a data processing center were begun. Under the direction of Ray Ashworth, the communication center was expanded and completely remodeled. The city was divided into eight radio communication zones, and calls from citizens were automatically routed to a dispatcher responsible for the part of the city from which the citizen was calling. Everett Leonard, a former FBI agent, created a comprehensive records system. Computer equipment and a new data processing system were installed which allowed for the storage and immediate retrieval of vital data.[54] The three systems became models which other law enforcement agencies would emulate.

The Chicago Police Department had never systematically collected crime statistics. As a consequence, the annual crime rate the department released to the media was not accurate. It was, in fact, considerably lower than it should have been. Wilson never considered doctoring crime statistics to win community support for his efforts. Quite the contrary. He informed the community that the department would, for the first time, accurately report crime information. He prepared citizens for a major increase in reported crime, which Wilson took great care to explain would be a statistical increase, not a real one.[55]

Serious crime went up 90.9 percent during 1960.[56] Wilson promised that it would level off now that the new system was in effect. Much to the superintendent's consternation, crime continued to rise at an alarming rate. Wilson ordered his staff to audit the new data processing machinery. They did, and discovered that offenses cleared by arrest were inadvertently being added to the total reported crimes category, thereby increasing by 25 percent actual crimes reported to the department. The error was corrected, and serious crime stabilized as O. W. had promised it would.

Many of the practices carried on by Wilson's predecessor generated special problems for him both in the department and in the community. For example, over the years, the dominant methods of police patrol had been three-wheel motorcycles and two-man cars. Wilson knew these types of patrol did not make maximum use of manpower. The superintendent discontinued the use of the three-wheel vehicles, added five hundred new cars to his motorized fleet, and manned most with one man, except at night in the areas with the highest rate of violent crime. It was not a popular move among the rank and file.[57] He also was forced to alienate a segment of the community when another police department practice of long standing had to be ended.

It had been a continuing policy of Chicago's Catholic churches to sponsor bingo games to raise money. Bingo was illegal. Under previous police commissioners, the Church was exempted from the gambling laws. Parish priests would simply write to the police commissioner, informing him of the date and place of their bingo games. The commissioner would then inform the appropriate district captain of the event, and ask him to assist in any way he could. When O. W. Wilson received the same request, he replied that bingo was a violation of the law. Since he had taken an oath to uphold the law, it was quite impossible for him to countenance violations of it. There was a flood of mail from the Catholic community protesting this posture, but the superintendent would not retreat from his position. The bingo controversy raged on until Superintendent Wilson's stand was supported by the influential Catholic leader, Albert Cardinal Meyer.[58]

Superintendent O. W. Wilson experienced no overt political interference during his first year in office. He had the unqualified support of the news media, and it appeared that a substantial majority of the community was pleased by his efforts, though rank and file veterans still openly opposed police reform. This was evidenced by a near riot involving two thousand policemen attending a meeting to protest his attempt to modify the disciplinary appeals system.[59] Through it all, however, Mayor Daley remained firm in his pledge to maintain a "hands off" policy on police administration. Wilson conferred frequently with Daley, largely for the purpose of allowing the superintendent to brief the mayor on proposed plans, which Wilson usually presented as a *fait accompli.*[60] Superintendent Wilson slowly gained a respect for the mayor. The questions he posed to O. W. were penetrating, perceptive, and to the point. He appeared to be genuinely committed to Wilson and his programs, to which he gave unqualified support. The mayor never interfered with Wilson, never counseled him to slow down, never failed to furnish him with the resources necessary to fulfill his mission. Moreover, Mayor Daley insulated his superintendent from the city's aldermen, many of whom were plainly distressed over the concept of police reform.[61]

Richard Daley's unqualified support of Wilson was not without its reward. Scarcely one year before, the mayor had been under attack from all quarters because of the Summerdale Scandal. Now, he was being linked with O. W. Wilson as a positive force for police reform. Wilson's successes were Daley's successes, for Mayor Daley had turned police autonomy into something of a civic virtue. The role of reformer was a new one for the mayor, but he assumed it easily, and blithely accepted the praise of a grateful community.

A full year had passed. Wilson had laid the superstructure of what he believed would eventually be a model police department. Nonetheless, he detected a serious flaw in its organizational structure, a defect which inhibited his complete control of police operations, while leaving the department vulnerable to the influence of politicians. The scheme by which police service was decentralized by district was viewed by Wilson as a debilitating weakness. It was a first priority of the superintendent to radically change this system, even though the political ramifications were potentially explosive.

As he entered his second year in office, O. W. Wilson had, at the very least, proved wrong the veteran captain who at the onset of his superintendency had predicted, "He won't last six months."[62]

9

THE CAPTURE OF CHICAGO

Superintendent O. W. Wilson's redistricting scheme was the product of nearly one year of planning. The objectives of the controversial concept were to eliminate unnecessary police districts, draft district boundaries that were based on tactical requirements rather than political considerations, and institute a procedure which would ensure that district commanders would be accountable to the superintendent, not to politicians. The final design of Wilson's new program was ready by the fall of 1961. A high priority was assigned to enlisting community support for it.

Richard McDonell, Director of the Planning Division, was delegated primary responsibility for implementing the idea. He was assisted by the IACP's Ray Ashworth. They recommended that the number of districts be reduced from thirty-eight to twenty. Chicago's citizens had been led to believe that the greater the number of district stations the more police protection they could expect to receive, so the superintendent embarked on a project to sell his plan to the public by reeducating them.[1] Wilson and his headquarters staff spoke to community groups, held press conferences, and issued news releases, all of which were designed to persuade citizens that the reform was necessary and desirable. Since Richard McDonell had been placed in charge of the plan, the superintendent decided that he should shoulder the major burden for telling Chicago's citizens about it.

McDonell went from neighborhood to neighborhood, speaking to every group who would listen to him, regardless of their size or influence. His message was that the aim of the redistricting program was to increase police protection, not decrease it. He explained that a district station was little more than an administrative component where officers reported to duty, and where short-term prisoners were incarcerated. Calls for police service were made to the communications center in the headquarters building, so that the district station had nothing to do with the basic layout of beats or with the deployment of men and vehicles. Citizens were informed that the elimination of a district represented a saving of eighteen officers, men who were assigned to administrative tasks in the station. Closing district stations meant that most of these men could be released to patrol duty, thereby increasing police coverage in high crime areas.[2]

During the community education phase of his scheme, Wilson received no overt political opposition to the plan. Many of the aldermen feared the idea and despised Superintendent Wilson because of it; however, they had become so concerned over his threat to immediately report to the press any attempt to exert political pressure on the department that they did not even approach Wilson about the impending reform.[3] Instead, the aldermen deluged Mayor Daley with complaints over how it would lead to a loss of political influence in the community. Daley stood by his superintendent on the issue. It may well have been that the mayor knew that police redistricting would have little impact on the operation of the Democratic political apparatus, for he had a virtual army of precinct workers whose community relationships and "get out to vote" programs would not be even slightly hindered by police district consolidation. Moreover, lessening the aldermen's control over police operations might be a political bonus if it ended some of the embarrassing disclosures of political interference in police affairs which had plagued the Democratic administration in recent years.[4] One critic of Mayor Daley described his support of redistricting as "the one real act of political courage in his administration."[5] In any event, Wilson received no political pressure from city officials to back down.

Chicago's citizens seemed to accept redistricting, with one major exception. The neighborhood encompassing the University of Chicago resisted the plan because it split into two districts a community which was racially integrated, and which had developed a strong sense of cohesiveness. Neighborhood leaders and university officials feared that redistricting could contribute to the loss of community identity which they had worked for years to achieve.[6] Wilson listened to their arguments and found them persuasive. He ordered McDonell to redraft the plan so that the University of Chicago's neighborhood would be left intact. The original twenty-district scheme was changed to twenty-one.

When it became clear that the community was not opposing redistricting, the superintendent informed department personnel and the media of his intention to change the districts' command-control structure. Under the existing procedure, all district commanders were captains, none of whom had been promoted to that rank during O. W. Wilson's tenure in office. The captaincy was a civil service rank, which meant that disciplinary action could be invoked only for cause, and that the recipient had a right to utilize the disciplinary appeal process. Wilson believed that he should have the unilateral right to fill the sensitive post of district commander with whomever he wished, and to replace or reduce in rank those whom he felt were not accomplishing their mission.[7] O. W. wanted the power to oust managers who lacked initiative or displayed disloyalty without having his action reviewed by an appellate authority.[8] As a consequence, he created by fiat a new rank, district commander.

The new district commander position was a rank exempt from civil service protection. In the organizational structure, it was inserted between the captains and deputy chiefs, and could be filled either by lieutenants or captains. The men who held these positions would retain civil service protection for the rank they held prior to their appointment as district commanders, but would be beholden and answerable only to the superintendent for their district commandership.[9]

Wilson selected his district commanders carefully, using psychological profiles which had been completed on eligible officers. He announced his reorganization plan on 22 November 1961 and the appointment of new district commanders on 17 December.[10] Only two of the newly selected commanders had previously supervised a district, which meant that thirty-six of the thirty-eight captains who had been serving in this capacity were replaced. Of the twenty-one men, five held the civil service rank of lieutenant.

A small group of police captains strenuously opposed the plan. Six captains anonymously threatened to resign over the issue.[11] They did not. The bases of opposition were that personnel with the civil service rank of lieutenant would now supervise captains, and former district commanders were being reduced in authority to shift commanders.[12] One angry captain stated, "If you think any captain wants to be flunky to a junior officer, you're badly mistaken." Sixteen captains filed suit against the department in an attempt to keep Wilson from assigning lieutenants over their heads.[13] It failed.

As an adjunct to redistricting, the superintendent withdrew all detectives from districts and assigned them either to the Detective Division in headquarters or to one of six decentralized headquarters; he removed policewomen from districts and placed them under supervision of the Youth Division; and he created a task force.[14] The task force, consisting of a surplus of officers gained from redistricting, was a highly mobile unit assigned to augment district patrolmen. They were deployed in high crime areas, based upon computer predictions of where they would be most needed. Their main job was preventive patrol, and they answered radio calls only when no one else was available.[15] The entire operation was supported by a fifty-officer canine patrol, foot patrols, and umbrella cars.

The umbrella cars were an invention of Tom Rogers, an assistant chief in Oakland, California, who had been brought to Chicago as a consultant. Rogers's assignment had been to evaluate the effectiveness of foot patrol beats, most of which were eliminated because of their inefficiency. With manpower freed from foot patrol duty, more squad cars were deployed in the field. These extra patrol units "floated" from beat to beat as regular patrol cars had to foresake patrol duty to answer calls. Thus, like the "umbrella defense" in football, the umbrella cars was a strategy designed to forestall attack by the opposition. In effect, they took over preventive patrol responsibilities until beat cars could return to that activity. According to Wilson, Rogers's umbrella car concept was the first of its type anywhere.[16]

The dominant method of police patrol in Chicago was now the one-man car. O. W. Wilson was convinced of its value, but reaction to it among the rank and file continued to be unfavorable. In order to reassure his men that one-man cars were desirable, Wilson had his staff conduct a study to evaluate the idea in operation. The result was a report which defended the one-man car as effective, economical, and safe. The investigation revealed that to convert the Chicago Police Department to all two-man cars would entail an expenditure of seven million dollars, and require 1,209 more police officers. The report stated that one-man patrols were safer than two-man patrols because policemen working alone tended to be more alert to danger.[17] Despite the report, the Chicago Patrolmen's Association continued to criticize it as hazardous and ineffective.[18] O. W. Wilson was never able to persuade his officers to support the one-man car idea, although his belief in the concept never wavered.

Superintendent Wilson continually modified the police department's technical service capacity to support operations in the field. More radio channels were added to the communications center. The data processing unti began producing daily crime summary printouts and special weekly and monthly analyses of criminal activity. Equipment was purchased which allowed crime victims to scan photographs of suspects on microfilm viewers.[19] Wilson's search for technical aids to assist policemen in the community was a never-ending one.

O. W. Wilson's off-duty hours were devoted largely to social activities in the community, where he was in great demand as a speaker and dinner guest. Since Wilson both enjoyed and looked on such undertakings as a part of official responsibilities, he accepted as many invitations as his busy schedule permitted.[20] Ruth and Orlando Wilson soon became a familiar sight at concerts, diplomatic dinners, charitable affairs, banquets, the symphony, and the ballet. Socially, Wilson ascended to a stratum unknown to previous police commissioners. Unlike his predecessors, the superintendent did not usually attend political rallies, wakes, testimonial dinners for ward committeemen, or similar events. His favorite activities were formal occasions, at which he could don black tie. Chicago's upper social class found the tall, scholarly, articulate superintendent an asset to any dinner party. Ruth also proved to be popular with socially prominent Chicagoans, as she became extensively involved in social activities and charitable work.

The Wilsons found themselves unable to adequately entertain guests at home because of the size of their house. It was simply too small. Ruth prevailed on her husband to consent to a relocation. He agreed, and the Wilsons set out to find a new home. They selected a large, seven-room apartment on Commonwealth Avenue which overlooked Lincoln Park and Lake Michigan. They took up residence in November 1961. A maid's room was converted into a study for O. W. It was furnished in a characteristically spartan way, with a large desk and a filing cabinet. Wilson would sit for hours in the privacy of his study, evaluating staff studies which he did not have time to review during working hours.[21] The new apartment also gave Mrs. Wilson an opportunity to engage in a project which had been neglected as a result of the Wilson's move to Chicago.

McGraw-Hill, O. W. Wilson's publisher, had for years attempted to entice him into revising *Police Administration.* Wilson's Hawaiian sabbatical was to be used for this purpose, but his unanticipated move to Chicago had interfered with the plan. O. W.'s formidable schedule as superintendent of police prohibited him from embarking on the revision, so that Mrs. Wilson, with her husband's blessing, decided to rewrite the text. As a former criminology student, and as O. W. Wilson's closest observer, Ruth felt that she could adequately reflect the superintendent's philosophy. Mrs. Wilson spent more than two years on the project, writing in the apartment's small pantry. Wilson refused to involve himself in any of the work. He would even decline to answer questions on the text. When the manuscript was finished, it was accepted by McGraw-Hill. Wilson finally agreed to look at the book's page proofs, but after a cursory inspection, in which one sentence was changed, he flatly declined to do more. The second edition of *Police Administration* was published in 1963. The book's dedication read: "To Patricia Anne, Dear Child, this book is yours." It was Ruth Wilson's way of thanking Patricia for the hours which were devoted to the book instead of to her.[22]

The revised text did faithfully mirror O. W. Wilson's philosophy and professional values. There was a heavy emphasis on the orderly principles of organization and planning; the scientific distribution of patrol forces; investigative specialization; the need for complete record keeping and radio communications; the requirements of training, inspection, and discipline; precise specifications for police equipment; and the constant need to maintain integrity in the ranks. Only one page was devoted to a discussion of one man versus two men in a patrol car. Mrs. Wilson did not realize when she wrote it that it would become the most controversial part of the text.[23] Social science data on leadership, group dynamics, employee relations, morale, motivation, and interpersonal relations was conspicuously absent from the book.

Wilson had made a decision early in his tenure to select a successor from within the ranks of the Chicago Police Department. He was convinced that it was better to select a Chicago policeman for the post, since the man would have the benefit of Wilson's personal tutelage on a day-to-day basis. The officer he selected was James Conlisk, the deputy superintendent in charge of field services. Conlisk, an intelligent man, was honest and loyal to the superintendent. He unhesitatingly followed orders and ran the Bureau of Field Services according to the instructions passed down from his superior. Deputy Superintendent Conlisk was a capable commander who functioned well under supervision, but who lacked the initiative and technical expertise of an Orlando Wilson. Conlisk's moderate success as bureau commander belied his inability to exercise independent judgment and firm leadership.[24] It is not known what specific qualities O. W. Wilson saw in James Conlisk. Nonetheless O. W. selected Conlisk as Chicago's next superintendent of police long before he had any intention of retiring.[25] To prepare Conlisk for the role he would some day fill, Wilson had the deputy at his side constantly, so that he could be trained for the superintendency.[26] James Conlisk was not destined to succeed in the job. The fact that O. W. Wilson was convinced that with expert instruction even a mediocre man such as Conlisk could be molded into a skilled administrator, furnishes an insight into Wilson's concept of police professionalization. To Wilson, leadership was important to any police department. Yet he felt that because of his reorganization efforts, the Chicago Police Department was irrevocably on the road to excellence. In short, the process of reform would never be reversed as long as his successors continued his programs and kept a steady hand at the helm. New superintendents, then, would not be required to be innovative, merely faithful to Wilsonian principles, which were self-perpetuating, in Wilson's view.

O. W. Wilson had a cynical view of the rank and file. He felt that they should be closely watched, lest they misbehave. It was a posture which had been fostered throughout his career and which had been reinforced by Frank Carey's resistance to reform, which was seen by the superintendent as disloyal but indicative of the mainstream of rank and file opinion. Since most of Chicago's policemen were uniformed officers assigned to patrol duty, Superintendent Wilson took steps to control their behavior in the community. He believed that as long as individual officers were allowed to exercise wide discretion in field encounters with citizens, there was too much room for misconduct and abuse of authority. Written policies, in the form of general orders, special orders, and training bulletins, were disseminated to patrol officers, who were expected to adhere to them strictly. A major purpose of these publications was to mandate specific procedures to be followed in all field situations. The limits of police discretion were narrowed by Wilson, who felt that if departmental policy was restrictive enough, misconduct on the part of patrolmen would be systematically reduced and in time eliminated. Most policies had the same format: a logical step-by-step procedure for handling police matters. This "by the numbers" approach was to become characteristic of O. W. Wilson's policy formulation process. It was a highly simplistic manner of narrowing the exercise of line officer discretion, by a man who viewed a patrolman's freedom of judgment as a potentially evil influence on police administration.

Wilson's policy on the preliminary investigative duties of uniformed officers clearly illustrates his objective in this regard, and his search to find and mandate the "one best way" to handle operational tasks. A Chicago Police Department training bulletin summarized sequentially the duties of patrol officers in investigations as follows:

> Proceed to the scene with safety and dispatch.
> Render assistance to the injured.
> Effect arrest of perpetrator.
> Locate and identify witnesses.
> Interview complainant and witnesses.
> Maintain scene and protect evidence.
> Interrogate suspects.
> Note all conditions, events, and remarks.
> Arrange for collection of evidence.
> Report incident fully and accurately.
> Yield responsibility to detectives.[27]

As O. W. Wilson ended his third year in office, the reform effort seemed to be paying dividends. The Communications Center, created two years before, had been extended to twenty-four radio consoles, employed a staff of 300, and served more than 1,400 police vehicles. A police cadet program, patterned after the Wichita Police model, was initiated.

During its first year of operation, sixty-two young men between the ages of seventeen and nineteen had been appointed Chicago police cadets. A suburban teletype network was installed which established communications between the Chicago Police Department and suburban law enforcement agencies.[28]

There was still widespread dissatisfaction with Wilson among veteran members of the police rank and file. However, Frank Carey's campaign to force Wilson from office had met with no success, so Carey abandoned it.[29] Chicago's civic organizations and newspapers were consistently heralding the superintendent for professionalizing the police department. Mayor Daley seemed pleased to share in the community's praise of law enforcement in Chicago. When O. W. Wilson's three-year contract expired in 1963, Daley reappointed him for "as long as I'm mayor, or as long as he wants the job."[30]

Although Wilson was experiencing some success in his reform effort, everything was not going smoothly for him. One of the most difficult problems O. W. Wilson was attempting to come to grips with was organized crime. It was well financed, deeply involved in both legal and extralegal enterprises, and of pervasive impact on civic affairs. Many politicians were beholden to organized crime members, though Wilson never believed Mayor Daley was. Wilson expanded his vice and intelligence divisions, while increasing surveillance of major crime figures. He felt that he could not adequately fight the crime confederation unless he was given the power to wiretap. Efforts to have the Illinois State Legislature pass a wiretap statute were unsuccessful.[31]

It is doubtful if O. W. Wilson's administration had any real effect on organized crime in Chicago. It was as deeply entrenched in the city during his tenure as it had been in previous administrations. Even Wilson once admitted that "we have made little progress in our efforts to prosecute the higher-ups in organized crime."[32] He was persuaded that his inability to convince the legislature of the necessity of employing wiretaps was a primary reason for this failure.[33] Of course, there were a myriad of other reasons, not the least of which was the tolerance that Chicago's citizens had traditionally displayed. It also is clear that Wilson's rivalry with J. Edgar Hoover did little to ameliorate the problem. Hoover provided aid grudgingly, and on at least one occasion actually used an FBI investigation into organized crime to embarrass the superintendent. The incident merits attention.

During the summer of 1963, Attorney General Robert Kennedy made a speech to a bar convention in Chicago, in which he implied that the Chicago Police Department was one of the most corrupt law enforcement agencies in the nation.[34] Kennedy offered no specific charges or supporting evidence.[35] Wilson, who was agitated over the speech, wrote a polite letter to the attorney general asking him to furnish whatever documentation he had so that the police department could investigate the matter. Kennedy acknowledged receipt of Wilson's letter but never replied further. When he received Superintendent Wilson's letter, though, the attorney general directed the Federal Bureau of Investigation to conduct an investigation into possible Chicago police corruption. A brief memorandum was prepared by agents in the Chicago field office. It alleged that high-ranking Chicago police officers were receiving payments from members of organized crime. The report was given to Attorney General Kennedy, who neither used it nor forwarded it to Wilson. It is not known precisely why Kennedy ignored the memorandum, but the document was a carelessly prepared report replete with innuendos, gross generalizations, unsupported allegations, and vague charges. It often referred to meetings between police officers and known criminals, giving the officers' rank, yet not their names. In all, forty-three Chicago policemen were supposed to be involved. The source of the investigators' information was "unnamed informants."[36]

In the spring of 1964, the memorandum was leaked to *Chicago Sun-Times* reporter Sandy Smith, even though it had been classified as "confidential." J. Edgar Hoover's practice of leaking to friendly journalists information which damaged rivals has been well documented by former FBI agent William Turner. In any event, Smith wrote a series of stories based on the memorandum. Superintendent Wilson was able to obtain a copy of the report from Frank Kiernan, chief of the Federal Prosecution Unit based in Chicago. He was distressed to learn that it contained such vague accusations. Nevertheless, he ordered Deputy Superintendent Joseph Morris to investigate the charges. Morris later reported that he could substantiate none of the accusations. Morris did find that, in at least one case, a Chicago detective whom the investigators had learned was meeting secretly with Mafia figures was in reality an undercover operative assigned to infiltrate the crime confederation.[37]

The superintendent asked for and received from Frank Kiernan an apology for the memorandum, which Kiernan described as based on "gossip and rumor." The *Chicago Tribune* implored Wilson to furnish them a copy of the memo so that they could reprint it and discredit Smith and the *Sun-Times.* The superintendent refused because he felt that too many innocent policemen could be hurt by such action.[38]

Although the incident caused Wilson some distress, it did not seem to seriously distract him from his duties. He launched Operation Crime Stop in 1964, a public relations campaign designed to enlist citizens support in preventing crime. A card containing instructions on how to report and react to crimes in progress was issued to citizens, who were signed up as "crime-stoppers." He streamlined procedures for processing and disposing of firearms.[39] The Police Department also began publishing a comprehensive annual report. After reading the report, Austin MacCormick chided his old friend for what he considered a serious flaw in its production:

> The only thing wrong with the report is that there are only two pictures of you in it; the one beside your letter to the Mayor, and the one on page 18 of you lecturing to the commanding officers in training. Only two pictures? You'll never get anywhere that way, my boy. J. Edgar would have had at least 17 in that report.[40]

O. W. attempted one last fence-mending effort with J. Edgar Hoover, though it was done with tongue in cheek. During the winter of 1964, Wilson was attending a police conference in Washington when he confronted Director Hoover at a dinner. It was at a time when rumors that Wilson would replace Hoover were particularly widespread. The rumors always amused O. W., for he did not have the slightest interest in the FBI. Still, he never denied them, possibly because he took some satisfaction in the discomfort such speculation probably caused his old antagonist. Hoover was sitting at his customary place at the head of the main table, with trusted companion Clyde Tolson at his side. O. W. Wilson was several seats away. When Tolson briefly excused himself, Wilson, who had consumed several relaxing cocktails, sat down next to the director. The assemblage looked on in stunned silence as O. W. remarked, loudly enough to be heard by all: "J. Edgar, what do you say we cut the shit." The director, obviously flustered, made an inaudible remark, then stalked from the room.[41] It is doubtful if the two ever spoke again.

A continuing source of frustration to O. W. Wilson was the direction in which the American court system seemed to be going. He believed that the Supreme Court had become so concerned with the rights of criminal defendants that it had brought about crippling restraints on police officers. Among the most damaging curbs, according to Wilson, was the exclusionary rule, under which evidence could be barred from state courts on federal constitutional grounds; case decisions limiting police officers' right to search premises; the Escobedo decision, which held that the police could not question a criminal suspect unless his attorney was present; and the Miranda decision, in which the right to legal counsel was extended to the initial point of custody.[42] Wilson was distressed over these restraints because, in his judgment, the extension of rights for criminal defendants had led to a lessening of rights for victims of crime. Hampered by Supreme Court restrictions, the police were hard-pressed to keep dangerous criminals from ravaging cities.[43] He castigated his former friend, Chief Justice Earl Warren, civil libertarians, and corrections officials for subscribing to a "philosophy of excuse," in which individuals were not being held accountable for their behavior.[44] In a call for a return to traditional values, Wilson held that:

> Criminality is a lack of discipline. Young people must be taught that there are certain rules they must comply with, that they must respect the rights of others ... I think we must get back to the philosophy of our forebearers who held the individual responsible for his acts.[45]

Wilson had a respect for the United States Constitution, but he was convinced that Supreme Court decisions were not consistent with any reasonable interpretation of that document. A strict constitutional constructionist, O. W. believed that the high court's decisions were affecting dramatically his responsibility to provide protection to the community he had sworn to serve. Yet, he enacted departmental policies mandating strict adherence to these new decisions. Wilson was never tempted to permit his officers to take shortcuts around these hated case decisions, for that would have violated O. W.'s strong sense of ethics. Still, in a style utterly out of character, O. W. openly criticized a court system which he sensed had betrayed the American people.[46]

Superintendent Wilson's public statements criticizing the criminal courts led to feelings of ambivalence among civil libertarians, many of whom were revulsed by his view of the criminal law revolution,[47] but who also admired him for his impeccable honesty, and for his police reform in Chicago.[48] When they criticized the superintendent's attempt to have a wiretap law enacted, he responded, condescendingly, in a way calculated to point out the naïveté of his opponents:

> The Syndicate does not reduce its plans or orders to writing. The plans are discussed orally, and frequently by telephone. We cannot permit the Syndicate to take over society.

Wilson also drew criticism from civil libertarians for his support of a stop-and-frisk law, though they backed his unsuccessful campaign for a strong gun-control law.[49] The dilemma O. W. Wilson posed to civil libertarians was exquisite. He was a constant critic of the Supreme Court and permissiveness in society, an advocate of what they thought were repressive laws. He also wished for a return to traditional American values.

Nevertheless, O. W. Wilson was not an easy person to attack. Unlike other American police administrators, such as J. Edgar Hoover, Philadelphia's Frank Rizzo, and Los Angeles's William H. Parker, Wilson could not easily be classified as a reactionary or a doctrinaire conservative. He was pro-gun control, had embarked on an energetic plan to recruit black and Puerto Rican policemen, and had initiated an aggressive police-community relations program. Moreover, no one could accuse him of being a racist. Still, the superintendent did test the tolerance of civil libertarians, as evidenced by his handling of the Richard Speck case.

In the summer of 1966, eight student nurses at South Chicago Community Hospital were found murdered in their townhouse apartment. Another girl had survived by hiding under a bed. Superintendent Wilson, shocked by the murders, brought all his technical and investigative resources to bear on the blood-spattered home. Crime scene technicians were able to lift a set of fingerprints from the interior of the townhouse, while a police artist drew a composite picture of the suspect, based upon information furnished by the survivor.[50] The fingerprints belonged to a twenty-four year old itinerant seaman named Richard Franklin Speck, who also fit the description given by the surviving student nurse. A murder warrant was issued for Speck, and a photograph of him was obtained by the Chicago Police Department. Since any delay in recapturing Speck might have led to other killings, or to his fleeing the country, Wilson decided to act decisively.

The superintendent's friend and legal advisor, Minor Keith Wilson, was out of town, so O. W. was proceeding without the counsel of his aide. Wilson called a press conference at which he released Speck's photograph and a full description, including information on his tattooed left arm which read "Born to Raise Hell." During the press conference, Wilson announced:

> This man is the killer. We have the physical evidence. As far as I am concerned, there is no question about it.[51]

Richard Speck was arrested the following day when he sought medical treatment for injuries sustained in the attack.[52] The Chicago Police Department was praised by the community and by the press, but the superintendent of police was criticized by civil libertarians, among them Supreme Court Justice Potter Stewart, who charged that his remarks had jeopardized Speck's right to a fair trial. Civic groups, public officials, university professors, and journalists jumped to Wilson's defense, and the controversy eventually subsided. To O. W. Wilson, it was simply another case of an unreasonable restraint on police action designed to protect citizens.[53] To civil libertarians, it was one of those recurring incidents which mitigated their enthusiasm for Wilson. On balance, however, Chicago's liberal community tended to support their superintendent of police.

Superintendent O. W. Wilson's reform of the Chicago Police Department appeared to peak in 1965. Statistics for the previous year indicated that Chicago's rate of Part I Crimes declined 3.1 percent, while the national crime rate rose 13 percent. Operation Crime Stop appeared to be paying dividends, as more than 4,500 arrests were directly attributable to citizen cooperation in reporting crimes.[54] A full-time community relations coordinator was employed, and police-community relations workshops were being conducted in each district. The workshops, held monthly, were devised to ease racial tensions and increase citizen support of law enforcement. If Wilson seemed to be changing the community's attitude toward the Chicago Police Department, there is some evidence which indicates that the attitude of supervisory police officers toward their agency was also improving.

In 1960, at the height of the Summerdale Scandal, a survey of Chicago police sergeants revealed that they had a very low opinion of the administration of the department. Five years later, a follow-up study showed a substantial increase in favorable attitudes toward the way in which the department was being run. The effects of introducing professional norms into the Chicago Police Department were evident in this dramatic shift in attitudes.[55]

Because of Chicago's apparent success at police reform, stories of O. W. Wilson's leadership were carried in most popular news magazines. John Lindsay, the newly elected mayor of New York City, offered O. W. Wilson the commissionership of the New York Police Department.[56] O. W. refused it. He did not particularly like Lindsay, a liberal; he had no intention of working for an administration which forced its police department to labor under the scrutiny of a citizen-dominated review board; and he did not wish to leave Chicago at this stage of his stewardship.[57]

Wilson's ability to achieve his reform objectives was directly related to his skill in selling his budgets to the Police Board, the City Council, and the mayor. His success in this regard was phenomenal. His 1966 budget of $103 million represented an increase of more than $12 million over the previous budget, and an almost $32 million increase over the 1960 budget.[58] The studious manner in which his budgets were prepared, and the way in which Wilson was able to tie even the most minor financial requests into a broad program of reform have previously been discussed. In addition, he utilized another tactic which had been unknown to previous police commissioners.

Each police budget was expected to contain "breakage," unexpended money carried over from one budget year to another. This carryover usually resulted from the department's inability to fill new positions until well after the fiscal year was under way. Thus, although a full year's salary would be appropriated for each new position, considerably less than a full salary would be paid because of late recruiting. In pre-Wilson days, the average breakage was between one and three million dollars. O. W. reversed the practice of turning back funds. As the fiscal year drew to a close, Wilson would expend his breakage on new personnel and equipment which had not been authorized by the City Council or the mayor.[59] Each year the Police Board would be disturbed to learn that instead of millions of dollars in carryover funds, the department would turn back $35,000 or less. Bill McFetridge was especially critical of the practice as he would annually chastise the superintendent for his extravagance. Wilson, however, never failed to spend his breakage. Mayor Daley may not have approved of this tactic, but he never rebuked his superintendent because of it.[60] The use of breakage represented one more way in which O. W. Wilson exercised control over his agency.

Through 1965, Superintendent Wilson's relationship with Mayor Richard Daley remained cordial. They continued to meet and confer often. Daley was supportive of O. W.'s activities; nevertheless, there were some indications that the mayor felt that Wilson was a bit too uncompromising and inflexible on even the smallest of issues, and that he tended to treat the city's elected officials with open disdain. If Mayor Daley had any misgivings about O. W., though, they were more than offset by a declining crime rate, the absence of exposés of police corruption, community confidence in a well-equipped, professional-appearing department, and the national publicity attracted by Wilsonian reform. O. W. Wilson seemed to be fulfilling the mandate the mayor had given him five years before, and the spotlight of popular acclaim was wide enough for two. It is inarguable that Mayor Daley loved his city. It is also irrefutable that he neither loved nor was devoted to O. W. Wilson. He needed Wilson, and used him to restore confidence in his beleaguered administration, and in the municipal government of Chicago. Daley was a man of strong beliefs, as was the superintendent. At no point during Wilson's first five years in office did they ever openly disagree on an issue about which both felt strongly. If they had, and Mayor Daley had pressed the matter, O. W. would have resigned. But it was inevitable that these two powerful personalities would eventually clash.

Mayor Daley attempted to interfere directly in what Wilson considered to be his realm on two occasions. The first was over a political matter. The Chicago Police Department traditionally furnished a contingent of about a hundred policemen to the office of the state attorney, an elected Cook County official. Wilson felt that the practice was unsound. Chicago policemen were being gratuitously furnished to a county officer, and the superintendent was able to exert no control over their actions. He decided to end the practice. Wilson believed that it would be best to wait until there was a change in administration so that he could eliminate the police contingent before a new state's attorney assumed office. Unfortunately for Superintendent Wilson, he ordered the practice terminated just after Daniel Ward had been elected state's attorney.[61] Ward, a Democrat, had won with strong Daley support. When Ward heard of Wilson's plan, he asked the mayor to intercede in his behalf. Mayor Daley asked his superintendent if he would continue the practice. Keith Wilson strongly counseled O. W. to stand by his decision, which was a sound one. The superintendent did not. To him, the matter was simply not important enough to pursue. The Cook County state's attorney was to get his Chicago policemen.[62] Wilson would later have cause to regret that decision.* The incident did not appear to negatively affect the cordial association between Daley and Wilson, but a social phenomenon was moving toward Chicago which would lead to the deterioration of a relationship which had been constructed of fragile material indeed.

In 1965, the civil rights movement came to Chicago in the form of a series of demonstrations and marches. Acts of civil disobedience protesting racial discrimination became commonplace. Mayor Daley was infuriated by the demonstrations. He believed that they were designed to generate bad publicity for the city, rather than to encourage social reform. He felt that the police should respond to even the slightest violations of the law by arresting transgressors and transporting them promptly to jail.[63] The mayor was not particularly concerned whether or not Chicago's policemen handled demonstrators gently. His attitude toward civil rights workers did not improve when they marched and picketed in his neighborhood.[64]

Unlike the mayor, O. W. Wilson was convinced that the demonstrations should be carefully handled by the police, with arrests made sparingly. He strongly disapproved of the way in which demonstrations had been policed in the South. He believed that Southern policemen had overreacted, had used excessive force in making arrests, had harassed and intimidated civil rights workers, and had generally acted unprofessionally. The superintendent knew that many of the tactics employed by demonstrators were deliberately provocative in order to arouse feelings among the police which would lead to an excessive response.[65] Wilson did not approve of civil disobedience, but he approved of police misconduct

*See page 128 for an account of the killing of two Blank Panther leaders.

even less. As a consequence, he instructed his police officers to carefully guard the rights of demonstrators, and to avoid making arrests if possible, even if they had to ignore minor violations of the law. Though it was not in character for Wilson to overlook technical violations of the law, he departed from his long-standing policy of strict enforcement because of a concern that to do so would mean an expenditure of manpower which would better be used in crowd control.[66] Furthermore, he was not about to assist the demonstrators in publicizing their cause at the expense of the Chicago Police Department. If Wilson had his way, Chicago would would not be another Selma or Watts.

As civil rights workers marched through Chicago, arrests were made sparingly. Massive numbers of people were not involved in the demonstrations, so more often than not, when marchers decided to sit in at a street or intersection, traffic was simply rerouted around them. This frustrated both the demonstrators, who were having trouble working up community interest in their efforts because of a lack of punitive police action, and Mayor Daley, who felt that the demonstrators should pay for their sins against Chicago.[67] The mayor's irritation toward Superintendent Wilson's permissiveness grew to outrage during an incident which occurred in the Loop.

At the height of rush hour traffic, a small group of Catholic nuns invited arrest by sitting in the intersection of Madison Avenue and State Street. Wilson had his men dutifully direct traffic around them, until they voluntarily left the scene some thirty minutes later. When Daley heard of the incident, he was livid with rage.[68] A ward leader described Daley's reaction to the incident:

> It was the most frustrating thing for him. He'd sit there blowing his stack and shouting that Wilson was a dumb sonofabitch because he wasn't doing anything about the marchers. God, how he would have loved to see Wilson take a job on the other side of the world.[69]

Mayor Daley immediately telephoned the superintendent and demanded an explanation of his policy of enforcement. Wilson patiently explained to the fuming mayor the bases for his department's conduct, but Daley would have none of it. In rather direct terms, he informed O. W. that he strenuously disapproved of such permissive police conduct, and that he felt that wholesale arrests should be made. Apparently, he did not give Wilson a direct order to pursue a different course of action, for the superintendent neither ended his policy of restraint, nor resigned, which is what such overt interference by the mayor would have meant. The incident caused a deterioration in the tenuous relationship between Wilson and Daley.

Although Daley did not approve of Wilson's handling of the demonstrations, civil rights leaders did. When Whitney M. Young, Jr., was asked what he thought of New York City police commissioner Michael J. Murphy, he responded by saying:

> He had his heart in the right place . . . However, he does not possess the socially perceptive and understanding manner in working with Negro leaders demonstrated by Orlando W. Wilson. If Chicago is spared a riot this summer it may be because of . . . the concern of Wilson. Wilson has done outstanding police work.[70]

No one knows for sure when O. W. Wilson decided to leave Chicago, not friends, family, colleagues, or subordinates. He did not confide in anyone precisely when he arrived at the decision. But, from all that is known about Wilson, it seems reasonable to assume that he probably began thinking seriously of terminating his arrangement with the city after the incident. Yet, though his days may have been numbered, he was to spend another two years in the superintendency. Moreover, he never lost respect for the mayor, as evidenced by the fact that he told his wife that he wanted to see Daley reelected for one more term before his retirement.[71]

In 1966, Martin Luther King came to Chicago. King had thus far concentrated his civil rights activities in the South, but he saw in Chicago fertile ground for pointing out that racism was not restricted to a single section of the country. So he came to a community which the year before had witnessed the Watts Riot, which was concerned that it might some day experience the same problem, and where whites generally viewed blacks as threats to their economic and physical security. Reverend King was planning a summer-long series of marches and demonstrations to protest racial discrimination in education, employment, and housing. O. W. Wilson looked on King's trip as a challenge. If Chicago's police officers could function well under what promised to be highly provocative conditions, then they would truly earn the title "professional."[72] Mayor Daley looked on King's trip with foreboding, yet Wilson seemed to view it with a degree of enthusiasm.[73]

Chicago had seen civil rights demonstrations the preceding year, but not ones of the size, scope, and intensity which Martin Luther King had planned for it. King always generated attention from police chiefs in the cities he visited, but he was unprepared for the kind of reception he would receive from Chicago's superintendent of police.

During the last week in January, Reverend King arrived in Chicago to initiate the planning phase of his demonstrations. Superintendent Wilson took the opportunity to invite him to police headquarters for a conference. It was there that King learned that more than 20 percent of the police force was black, that there were ten black captains and three black district commanders, that the squad cars were being integrated, that the department was embarked on an ambitious program to improve its relations with the black community, and that the superintendent of police had displayed tolerance toward previous civil rights demonstrations.[74]

King spent the better part of the morning conferring with the superintendent, following which he was invited to address sixty high-ranking officers in the department's auditorium. He spoke for approximately forty minutes, telling the assemblage that Chicago had been selected as a target area because "conditions are bad here and we are here to prevent another Watts." He warned the group that civil disobedience would occur, but that he had urged his followers not to abuse police officers who made arrests. He explained that his plan was to begin slowly, with rent strikes and school boycotts, then move on to "more massive action" in the form of marches. He closed by saying:

> This is the first meeting I've had with any police department in the Nation. The only other times I faced groups of policemen, I was thrown in jail.[75]

Following his speech, Reverend King answered questions from the audience. The police commanders were subdued. While some may have been inwardly hostile, their queries were polite. They were curious about the specific tactics he would employ, whether he would continue his nonviolence, and where he intended to march.[76] Several captains warned him that if he or his aides violated the law, they would be arrested. He said that this was precisely what he wanted to occur. When King had finished answering questions, he and his wife went to Wilson's office, where they had coffee with the superintendent.[77] It was the first time Reverend King had ever been afforded such hospitality by a police administrator, and well before it was fashionable to do so.

The Kings spent the rest of the morning with Keith Wilson, touring police headquarters. They were shown the communications center, the data processing apparatus, and the various investigative offices. In one large office, a secretarial pool was busily at work typing reports. Most of the secretaries were black. King turned to Keith Wilson, smiled, and asked if he was concerned that a white civil rights organization might file suit against the police department for racial discrimination. Before King had left for the day, he promised O. W. Wilson that the Chicago Police Department would be notified in advance of the location of all demonstrations, the number of people who would be involved, and the tactics which would be used.[78] In a later press conference, he lauded Superintendent Wilson "for showing a concern for doing the right thing, and for letting his aides know what is taking place in this country."[79]

Instead of being treated like an intruder, the Reverend Martin Luther King was accorded treatment generally reserved for distinguished visitors which, in Wilson's view, he was. However, he was not immediately invited to City Hall. Outwardly, Mayor Daley refused to attack the civil rights leader, but privately he criticized him as a "rabble-rouser, a trouble-maker."[80] He saw King as a subversive, a man who was being financed by left-wing elements committed to disrupting America's institutions.[81] Three months after Dr. King's meeting with O. W. Wilson, Mayor Daley summoned him and members of the Southern Christian Leadership Conference (SCLC) to a meeting in his office. King told Daley that Chicago was not making enough progress in ending racial discrimination. He promised a full summer of demonstrations. Daley, in front of television cameras, and with reporters taking notes, had several city officials discuss the programs which the city of Chicago was implementing for poor people. The mayor's objectives were to publicly endorse King's goals, to show that the city had an on-going program of social reform, and to undercut King's impact on the community. King and Daley parted that day, outwardly cordial. Each was convinced, however, that the other was an evil man.[82]

As the summer of 1966 approached, Martin Luther King was constantly in the news as he attempted to mobilize blacks and sympathetic whites for his demonstrations. He continued to plan for nonviolent civil disobedience, while warning the community that Chicago had all of the racial problems which had led to the Watts Riot.[83] Mayor Daley tried to counter King's statements with press releases proclaiming his administration's concern for racial equality. Meanwhile, O. W. Wilson was implementing a training program to impress on the police rank and file that they must be prepared to delicately handle the demonstrations which were coming.

Wilson released a directive which explicitly prohibited verbal abuse of citizens. The policy pronouncement, which was widely circulated in the law enforcement community, and which was ultimately adopted by hundreds of other police departments across the country, actually listed racial terms that no American police administrator had ever publicly acknowledged existed. The policy, in typical, "by the numbers" style, read:

At all times departmental personnel will:
1. Never show any bias or prejudice against race, religion, or any other group or individual.

2. Act, speak, and conduct themselves in such a manner as to treat all persons with complete courtesy and with that respect due to every person as a human being.
3. Never talk down to any group or individual or engage in the use of derogatory terms such as "Nigger," "boy," "Wop," "Kike," "Chink," "Shine," "burrhead," "Dago," "Polack," "Bohunk," and the like.[84]

The summer of 1966 came, and the streets of Chicago were filled with chanting, singing, praying civil rights demonstrators,[85] led by Martin Luther King, who, true to his word, closely cooperated with the police. Before each march, the police were apprised of its route, the number of marchers, and their destination. Riot equipped officers ringed the demonstrators as they wound their way through Chicago. The cooperation between the SCLC and the Chicago Police Department was so close that, on an occasion when organizers had given too little warning to Wilson of a planned march, and had underestimated the number of demonstrators, the superintendent's criticism of their failure to keep him adequately briefed was met with a quick apology.[86]

At first, King led his marches through the routes traditionally followed by demonstrators: the Loop, business districts, the Civic Center, ghetto neighborhoods. Black rioting broke out in Chicago's West Side as the temperature rose above 100 degrees. It lasted several days, but was put down by policemen and National Guardsmen. Mayor Daley, in an oblique reference to Martin Luther King, blamed it on "outsiders."[87] Wilson's policemen acted with restraint. The cries of "police brutality" which customarily followed such police action were absent.[88] One month after the riot, Martin Luther King switched tactics, as he informed city officials that he intended to lead marches through white working-class communities.

King's marchers wound through heavily Catholic sections populated by people of Polish, Italian, Irish, and Lithuanian ancestry. They walked through bungalow sections in Gage Park and Cragin, and into nearby Cicero, as residents lined the streets, hurling invective, obscenities, rocks, and bottles.[89] All the while, Chicago's policemen protected demonstrators from harm, as they situated themselves between marchers and residents. Many police officers assigned to crowd control duty were members of the same communities through which they were escorting demonstrators, and they shared both religion and ancestry with the residents. If they felt resentful toward the marchers and sympathetic toward the blue-collar inhabitants, it did not affect their conduct in the field. Wilson had given strict orders to protect the demonstrators, and police supervisors were held precisely accountable for the actions of their subordinates.[90]

During a march through Gage Park, Martin Luther King was struck by two rocks, and was narrowly missed by a thrown knife. More than 1,200 policemen battled a crowd of 5,000 as they besieged some 700 marchers. After five hours, 45 residents had been arrested, as the remainder were dispersed. Cries of "police brutality" were heard, but this time they were being uttered by white people. In a bizarre reversal of roles, a plea for the creation of a police review board was attacked by a prominent black civil rights leader as unnecessary as long as Wilson was in command of the police department.[91]

In an effort to cool community passions, the superintendent made a public appeal to Chicago citizens. He told them that the demonstrators had a right to march, as long as they did not violate the law, and that the police force was not taking sides. Wilson asked residents to help their police officers by adhering to the following rules:

1. At any demonstration, obey requests of officers who tell you to move away or leave the area.
2. Do not aid troublemakers by heckling or harassing demonstrators or the police.
3. Stay away from demonstrations or marches; if caught in such an area, leave quickly.
4. Keep your children away from demonstrations or marches.
5. Don't risk a police record by failure to follow police instructions.[92]

Mayor Daley felt the demonstrations, and the residents' reaction to them, were embarrassing the city. He was in constant meetings with subordinates trying to find a way to end the marches.[93] There is not evidence to indicate that he was dissatisfied with Wilson's handling of them, or that he tried to directly interfere with the superintendent.

As the marches threatened to break into full-scale racial rioting, city officials met with Martin Luther King in a "summit conference," at which an agreement was reached which pledged the city to an aggressive antidiscrimination program.[94] By fall, King had departed, and the city returned to a relatively normal state.

O. W. Wilson was not sorry to see Dr. King leave Chicago. The demonstrations had been costly and time consuming, and they had forced the police department to forsake many of its normal activities, including preventive patrol. Still, Wilson respected King, whom he saw as a courageous man committed to high ideals. The superintendent felt that King had a right to march and demonstrate, and although Wilson did not approve of civil disobedience, he admired King's willingness to pay the price for his acts.[95]

As 1967 approached, Mayor Daley began campaigning for reelection.

His Republican opponent was John L. Waner, a wealthy businessman who had been Senator Charles Percy's campaign manager. Waner, a liberal, campaigned on a platform of improved social programs, better housing for blacks, a quality education for young people, and honesty in government.[96] Almost as an afterthought, Waner promised to fire O. W. Wilson because he had become too independent of supervision from public officials. Daley acknowledged Waner's claim of police independence, pointing out that this was a virtue rather than a vice.[97] Of all the issues in the campaign, Waner's pledge to dismiss Wilson generated the widest media coverage. Waner was later to complain:

> When I talked about important issues, they ignored me. When I said I'd fire one guy, it got me the biggest headline of the day. It was very frustrating.[98]

O. W. Wilson stood aloof from the election. His sympathy was with Daley, but he never publicly spoke out. John Waner's anti-Wilson stance failed, as Mayor Daley won a plurality of some 500,000 with 73 percent of the vote.

For O. W. Wilson, it was now time to retire. The basis for his decision to leave Chicago has been a subject of some controversy. For example, Mike Royko has theorized that Mayor Daley forced O. W. out because of a desire to again grasp control of the police department.[99] Daley, a man who was not fond of sharing power, had almost completely delegated the authority to administer the police department for some seven years. It is clear that despite the political dividends that Wilson's superintendency had meant to the mayor, he was becoming increasingly disenchanted with Wilson's independence. Perhaps O. W. had stayed on longer than Daley had anticipated, and the mayor, recently elected by his biggest margin ever, felt that it was now politically feasible to oust Wilson. Certainly from all that is known about O. W. it is clear that even if he was forced from office, he would not have publicized the fact. Yet, Royko's theory, while based on some circumstantial evidence, is chiefly speculation.

After reviewing the facts surrounding Wilson's resignation, the author has rejected Mike Royko's theory, which has too many incongruities to be valid. Mrs. Wilson contends that her husband's retirement came in the wake of a health problem. Wilson was experiencing a tremor in his right hand which, at times, was uncontrollable. It was affecting his handwriting and causing him some public embarrassment. The tremor, which was hereditary, had become progressively worse. It forced him to clasp his hands together during press conferences to hide the shaking.[100] Wilson was a proud man to whom such a malady would have taken on great significance. He had always taken pride in his handwriting and in his public image, both of which were now being affected.

In addition to his health, Wilson was sixty-seven years old, had just seen the mayor reelected, and had watched his own reform efforts bear fruit. These facts, when weighed with several others, tend to discredit Royko's thesis. In both Fullerton and Wichita, Wilson had bowed out gracefully, without recrimination or public outcry. Nevertheless, though he did not outwardly criticize city officials in either community, he never praised them either. His most private correspondence contained criticism of both city administrations. Such was not the case in Chicago. He remained a supporter of Mayor Daley, did not criticize the mayor to his most trusted associates, and even returned to Chicago in 1971 to speak in support of Daley's reelection bid.[101] If the mayor had forced Wilson to resign, everything in his background indicates that he would have simply faded away, quietly; but that he would never have uttered a good word about Daley in the process. So, as a result of these factors, the author believes that O. W. Wilson's retirement was voluntary; the result of age, infirmity, years of service, and a personal desire to devote much of his remaining life to his family.

On 16 May 1967, Wilson took the occasion of his sixty-seventh birthday to formally announce his retirement. He resigned in a brief letter to Mayor Daley, in which he stated:

Today, as you know, is my 67th birthday. This seems an appropriate occasion to announce formally to you my decision to retire from the Chicago Police Department, effective August 1, 1967. I plan to take my annual furlough, beginning July 1, at which time I shall terminate my active services as superintendent. It is my belief that the programs initiated slightly more than seven years ago for the reorganization of the police department are firmly established. There is an excellent core of leadership in the department to continue this leadership. All ranks of the department have contributed to a successful reorganization of the department, and the high morale of these officers encourages me to believe that they will maintain the high standards for which we have labored.[102]

Wilson personally delivered the letter to Mayor Daley, who acknowledged the resignation "with a sense of personal and civic loss."[103] He forwarded a one-paragraph letter to Wilson congratulating him on his birthday. On the bottom of the letter, Daley wrote, almost as an afterthought: "Thanks for all your help in making Chicago a better city."[104]

The outpouring of praise for the superintendent following his retirement announcement was unprecedented in Chicago police history. The media, businessmen, civil libertarians, corporate officers, public officials, and ordinary citizens all joined in the accolades. John S. Boyle, presiding judge of the Circuit Court, called Wilson "not only the finest police superintendent in the United States, but perhaps the finest in the world." Governor Otto Kerner said Wilson "has left behind a legacy of outstanding law enforcement." George Mahin, director of the Better Government Association stated, "Wilson has performed a tremendous service. . . ." When Edwin Berry, director of the Chicago Urban League heard of the retirement, he said, "I'm kind of speechless. We are all very cognizant of the work O. W. has done." The Chicago administrator for Martin Luther King's Southern Christian Leadership Conference termed Wilson "in the upper category of police executives."[105] State Senator Russell Arrington said, "Wilson has won the respect of all law enforcement bodies in the country. Public service in Illinois is better off because O. W. Wilson came to Chicago." The president of Chicago's Bar Association, William McSwain, termed Wilson's tenure "an outstanding job. His resignation will be a great loss." A week after his retirement announcement, radio station WLS broadcast a statement every four hours, for a full day. An excerpt read: "Thank you, Mr. Wilson. And all Chicagoans can say, we're glad we knew him. Chicago is better because of his efforts." The *Chicago American* titled a half-page tribute to Wilson "From Summerdale to Superiority." The *Chicago Tribune* stated that Wilson had "boldly met the challenge." The *Kansas City Star* editorialized that Wilson "took a rinky-dink police department—sloppy, corrupt and clownish—and fashioned it into a respected major leaguer." A Chicago patrolman wrote his superintendent, "Our image is still growing, we hold our heads high with great pride, we challenge our critics . . . Thank you." A half-page cartoon in the *Chicago Sun-Times* depicted a nightstick and a badge talking. The nightstick said, "I stand a little straighter," and the badge replied, "I shine a little brighter."[106]

O. W. Wilson recommended as his successor Deputy Superintendent James Conlisk, Jr. The recommendation miffed the Police Board, for it alone had the authority to make such pronouncements, and it felt that O. W.'s announcement had placed them in the uncomfortable position of either accepting Conlisk, and making it appear as though it were a rubber stamp for Wilson, or ignoring the last wish of a popular superintendent.[107] They selected the former alternative.

Several farewell parties were held for the Wilson family by a community grateful for the service of their superintendent of police.

10

ORLANDO'S HIDEAWAY

The Wilsons made plans for a leisurely trip to southern California. O. W. felt none of the urgency to arrive hurriedly, a characteristic of so many of his other travel plans. He arranged to have all the family furniture packed and shipped west, while booking passage for Ruth, Patricia, and himself on a train to San Diego. The *Chicago Daily News* found symbolic meaning in the fact that the train on which the retired superintendent was to travel was the Sante Fe Railroad's "Super Chief."[1]

There was one last party for O. W. At the railroad station, a large gathering of well-wishers, including Acting Superintendent James Conlisk, met to bid the Wilsons farewell. O. W. cut three cakes provided for the occasion, each of which spelled out his initials, O. W. W. Conlisk made a brief speech praising his predecessor's contribution to law enforcement, and promising not to make major changes in the police department, a pledge he would not fulfill. Wilson then said goodby to the assemblage, after expressing full confidence in Conlisk.[2] When asked by a reporter what he would miss most about Chicago, Wilson facetiously replied, "the press." On the evening of 30 June 1967, the Super Chief pulled from the Dearborn Street Station with an O. W. Wilson who was looking forward to retirement.[3]

The Wilsons settled in Poway, a rural community located in the foothills of San Diego County. O. W. selected his new home with the same precision that had marked his professional career. He wanted privacy, a place where Patricia could enjoy the outdoors, enough yard for a garden, and room in the house for a den. He also wished to live close to his brother and sister. He secured a map of the region, drew a circle which represented a twenty-five mile radius of his sister's home, then set out to house hunt in that area.[4]

The Poway house, termed by the press "Orlando's Hideaway," fit all those requirements. It was a four-bedroom ranch house situated on one acre. It had a pool and a small citrus orchard. He converted one of the bedrooms into a study; another was turned into a work room for Ruth.[5]

O. W. Wilson approached retirement in much the same way that he had confronted other challenges: totally, and with vigor. He had devoted his best effort to police administration, and he was convinced that history would record him as the greatest law enforcement scholar and administrator since Vollmer.[6] Nevertheless, all that was in the past. Wilson was retired now, and to O. W. retirement meant that he had divorced himself from the police service. During his first year in Poway, he received literally hundreds of offers to return to law enforcement, as a teacher, administrator, or consultant. He refused all, usually bluntly. Wilson developed a stock reply to requests for his service: "I will not do anything inconsistent with the aims of my retirement." Even an offer to lecture at a local high school class on law enforcement was turned down.[7]

The fact that O. W. was now in retirement did not deter his old nemesis, J. Edgar Hoover, from taking one last retributive measure against him. At the 1967 convention of the International Association of Chiefs of Police, a motion was made nominating O. W. as a Distinguished Service Member of the IACP. A Distinguished Service Award is the highest honor which the association can bestow on a member.[8] It is given to those police administrators who have "made an outstanding contribution to the science of police administration...." Few men have received it.[9] In order to become a Distinguished Service Member, the executive committee of the IACP must unanimously recommend a candidate to the general membership, who then must approve the nominee by a two-thirds vote.[10] When Wilson's name came before the executive committee, it produced a positive reaction among the delegates, several of whom made complimentary speeches. No one criticized the nomination. When the balloting was taken, the result was forty-nine votes for the nomination, none opposed, and one abstention. Since a unanimous vote was required, the single abstention killed the Wilson nomination. It was cast by Joe Casper, the assistant director of training for the FBI. Although there was anger over the incident among the IACP rank and file, O. W. Wilson never expressed the slightest concern over it.[11]

Despite his initial refusal to become actively involved in police work, O. W. Wilson never lost enthusiasm for and interest in his profession. Each morning he would sit at the kitchen table and read the newspaper from cover to cover, except the sports section. Every evening, he would dutifully watch Walter Cronkite on the CBS News. He was especially concerned with police-related news.[12] He also subscribed to the major police journals in order to keep abreast of the latest technological developments in the field.

Law enforcement was becoming increasingly newsworthy, with the police coming under fire for their handling of riots and demonstrations. O. W. was consistently asked by the media to comment upon the situation, but he rarely did. In 1968, he watched with dismay the televised accounts of the Democratic National Convention in Chicago. He saw Chicago police officers beating demonstrators with nightsticks, breaking crowd control formations to attack people, and generally acting like an untrained rabble. Wilson was appalled by their behavior. He sympathized with his former subordinates because of the provocative tactics employed by demonstrators; however, Wilson believed that the true test of a police officer was whether he could act professionally in the face of extreme provocation. The Chicago police failed this test dismally, and the retired superintendent was angered and disappointed by their failure.

One evening, following a particularly bloody confrontation between officers and demonstrators, Mayor Daley called O. W. to ask his opinion of the situation. Wilson told Daley that policemen had used excessive force in dealing with demonstrators, and that they should be prohibited from any further excesses. He called for closer supervision of individual officers. Wilson also implored Daley to have Superintendent Conlisk show officers a training film on the use of the baton which O. W. had made during his tenure.

Wilson saw no improvement in the conduct of the Chicago police, despite his conversation with the mayor. He was disappointed that it was Mayor Daley who called, and not Superintendent Conlisk, whom he blamed for the debacle. Conlisk had not prepared them for the demonstrations properly and had not exerted firm control over his policemen. Conlisk had not resisted the mayor's influence on the department's preparations for the demonstrations. Yet, O. W. never faulted Daley. He felt that Mayor Daley was filling a void created by the absence of strong leadership on the part of the superintendent. Since Daley was a politician, he could not be expected to fully comprehend the intricacies of police administration, and the ramifications of loosely controlled police action. He therefore acted in the way any layman would under the same circumstances, and reacted to criticism defensively, the way any experienced politician would. Wilson knew that if he had been superintendent during the convention, his policemen would have acted professionally, with poise and restraint in the face of provocation.[13] It was the superintendent's job to administer police service in the city of Chicago. If that service was less than adequate, then it was the superintendent who should be blamed, not the mayor.

The demonstrations, coupled with reports Wilson was receiving from Chicago, began to convince him that James Conlisk's superintendency was a failure. Conlisk had disbanded Wilson's Inspections Division, while diluting the authority of the Internal Affairs function. He had also allowed the mayor to interfere with the day-to-day operations of the police department.[14] In 1969, O. W. received a letter from Karl Detzer, a roving editor for *Reader's Digest.* Detzer obliquely criticized Conlisk by telling Wilson "you set too fast a pace for the poor guy."[15] In 1972, his former director of Public Information, Mel Mawrence, reported that "morale is so low in the CPD that the officers do little or less than what they have to do. . . ."[16] By this time, O. W. Wilson had reached the unhappy decision that he should never have selected James Conlisk as his successor. Wilson never questioned Conlisk's loyalty or honesty, but he belatedly subscribed to Ruth's notion that Conlisk was a weak man who avoided difficult judgments and who displayed few of the traits of leadership necessary to succeed as a police administrator.[17] Why Wilson had made such an error in judgment is open to speculation. Ruth Wilson believes that her husband put too great a value on the fact that Conlisk had held a high position with the Chicago Police Department in the previous administration. In essence, he felt that anyone who had attained such a position of prominence and had remained honest in the face of temptations to do otherwise, was worthy of the superintendency. Had Wilson used more rational factors in his decision making, Conlisk might not have been his choice. In any event, it is clear that during his last years, O. W. Wilson looked on James Conlisk as one of his greatest failures in forty-six years of law enforcement service.

In the winter of 1969, an incident occurred which must have caused Wilson to reevaluate another of his decisions. During the first week of December, a squad of Chicago policemen assigned to the state's attorney's office raided an apartment at 2337 Monroe Street. The apartment was occupied by two Black Panther leaders, Fred Hampton and Mark Clark, who were killed in a hail of police bullets. The investigation which followed eventually led to charges that the state's attorney had covered up the truth in an effort to justify the killings. Indictments were returned against several policemen and the state's attorney.[18] It must have given Wilson pause to reflect on the wisdom of the advice he had been given by Minor Keith Wilson, who years before had implored O. W. to withdraw Chicago policemen from the state's attorney's office.[19] During the Black Panther investigation, Superintendent Conlisk refused to force his men to undergo a polygraph examination when their credibility was called into question. Wilson was so distressed by the refusal that he submitted to a rare interview, in which he stated: "the State's Attorney's police are, first of all, Chicago policemen, and . . . I don't see any reason why lie detector tests shouldn't be given."[20]

If Orlando Wilson had cause to reevaluate the appropriateness of several of the decisions he had made during his professional career, there is no evidence to indicate that he had the slightest misgivings over his general philosophy of law enforcement, or over the road he believed policemen must travel to professionalize.[21] Policemen must be honest, devoted to community service, well-educated and trained, and courteous. Police departments must be free of politics, and organized along military lines. Police administrators must exert firm discipline over their personnel, brook no interference from politicians, be willing to employ advanced technology, and be prepared to deploy men and material according to a scientifically developed plan. His commitment to these ideas never wavered, as evidenced by the publication of the third edition of *Police Administration*.

Because of the incredible financial success of *Police Administration*, McGraw-Hill asked Wilson to update the text. At first, he refused. The task was more than the retired Wilson wished to undertake. He later relented when it was suggested that he find a co-author. The man he selected to assist in the revision was Roy C. McLaren, a former criminology student at Berkeley and director of the Field Services Division of the IACP. Wilson remembered McLaren as a competent writer. In addition, McLaren's position with the IACP had allowed him to keep abreast of the latest ideas in law enforcement. O. W., in characteristic terseness telephoned Roy McLaren at home and said: "Roy, this is O. W. Wilson. I'd like to have you co-author the third edition of *Police Administration*. Will you do it?" The answer was "yes," and they embarked on the project in late 1969. The agreement was that Wilson would receive two-thirds of the royalties, with McLaren receiving one-third.

Roy McLaren did most of the work. O. W. primarily rewrote the material in the second edition which had become outdated. Much of the new material was from either the Chicago Police Department or from police agencies which McLaren had surveyed with the IACP. The third edition was published in 1972. It fairly represented Wilson's view of politics, personal integrity, professionalization, community relations, organization, technology, civil service, and unions. Twelve thousand copies were sold in its first year, grossing approximately $150,000.[22]

Although O. W. Wilson was comfortably retired in Poway, he was disturbed over the upheaval which the country appeared to be undergoing. Black rioting, student revolt, war protest—all served to impress on Wilson that the nation was in turmoil. The political assassinations seriously troubled him. When, in response to the Martin Luther King murder, a a friend remarked, "It's about time," Wilson chastised her for callousness. He was confident that the malaise which gripped the country was a temporary phenomenon, but the factor which most distressed him was the apparent rebellion against authority. Wilson had an admiration bordering on awe for those in positions of authority, whom he believed should be permitted to pursue their programs unhindered by political interferences so long as they remained scrupulously honest and truthful. For example, O. W. was not a champion of the Vietnam War; however, he did feel that the president should be allowed to conduct the war unhampered by the inhibiting influences of protesting citizens and dissident congressmen.[23] Wilson's posture on this issue was probably colored by his experience as a police executive. He had been a strong administrator, not prone to share with subordinates his responsibility to make unilateral policy decisions. Although O. W. knew that citizens and congressmen had the right to exert an influence on public policy, he sympathized with the beleaguered president. Wilson had been in command of organizations when external pressure forced him to divert his attention from administrative duties, and he knew how difficult it must have been for the president of the United States to function with maximum efficiency under similar conditions. O. W. empathized with the president as a fellow administrator. He gave little thought to the processes which make democratic institutions different from all others. It was not a very democratic posture, but O. W. Wilson had never been a very democratic administrator.

O. W. had been accustomed to a high-powered way of life in Chicago, where activities were carefully planned to make use of all his time. Though his life in Poway was a more leisurely one, this penchant for orderliness and organization continued. Each morning, Wilson would rise early, to the same breakfast of two eggs, bacon, toast, orange juice, and coffee. The day was divided logically. He had carefully measured a one and one-half mile pathway from his home. Each morning and afternoon he would take his walk, exactly at the same time. O. W. maintained his considerable yard, with the help of a neighborhood boy. He also tended a small garden, which was perfectly rectangular. The rows were precisely measured, and the watering was studiously applied in the same daily amounts. O. W.'s garden was not tended, in the traditional sense. It was administered in the Wilsonian sense.

Wilson also read voraciously. He preferred books on history, yet his taste even ran to mystery novels. He enjoyed books by Agatha Christie, or others which had a "who-done-it" theme. O. W. never bothered with novels in which the hero was larger than life and employed extreme physical violence. He completely disdained Mickey Spillane books and their ilk. Most of his reading was done in the study, which Mrs. Wilson had forced him to adorn with the awards and trophies won during nearly one-half century of law enforcement service.

O. W. devoted a good deal of his retirement to the family. Mrs. Wilson had expressed interest in writing a biography of a western mountain man, so he invested the better part of a summer to assisting Ruth in her research. O. W., Patricia, and Ruth drove through Arizona, New Mexico, Wyoming, Texas, and northern California in pursuit of data. When O. W. was at the wheel, he would drive directly to their destination of the day: no stops, no side roads, no sightseeing, no deviations from the travel plan—much to the consternation of his family, who occasionally found O. W. just a bit too well-organized.[24]

In the fall of 1971, Wilson went to his physician for an annual physical examination. The doctor discovered that he had a tumor on his lung. Wilson was admitted to a local hospital, where surgery was performed to remove a portion of the upper lobe of one lung. His recovery was speedy and apparently complete.[25]

O. W. had recuperated from the surgery so quickly that his doctor permitted him to go on a Mexican trip with friends. He left in the spring of 1972 and spent nine days leading a group through the rugged mountains of Chihuahua, sightseeing and collecting trinkets.[26]

When Wilson returned home from Mexico, he seemed overly fatigued. He complained of a general feeling of weakness, and for the first time in his adult life began taking afternoon naps. His appetite diminished. Slowly, he lost weight. After several months, his health had deteriorated to the point that he could neither dress nor feed himself. On the morning of 18 October 1972, O. W. rose early, dressed himself for the first time in months, walked into the living room, and opened the drapes. Then, as Patricia and Ruth looked on, he sat in his favorite chair, where he died peacefully of a stroke.[27]

O. W. Wilson's funeral was open only to family and selected friends. Messages of sympathy came from around the world. His obituary was printed in scores of newspapers, including the *New York Times* and the *London Times*. When Roy McLaren wrote a full-page obituary of Wilson in the *Police Chief,* he stated:

To the police of the world, the loss of O. W. Wilson will be immense. Internationally, he was widely known as the greatest authority in the history of police administration. In the United States, only August Vollmer, Bruce Smith, and J. Edgar Hoover approached him in stature as an influence for good in American law enforcement.[28]

11

CONCLUSION

American law enforcement has had its teachers, researchers, philosophers, authors, administrators, and consultants. Some of the men who filled these roles have made a substantial contribution to the police service and to its literature. The factor which distinguished Orlando Winfield Wilson from other noted police authorities was that he was deeply involved in all the aforementioned undertakings. For example, Los Angeles Chief of Police William H. Parker reversed the course of a single agency and assumed a position of leadership for law enforcement in southern California; J. Edgar Hoover's influence, despite his continuing attempt to achieve immortality as the patriarch of law enforcement, was really quite narrow, and not particularly innovative except in the field of training; but Wilson's influence was pervasive. He changed the face of police administration through his teachings, publications, consultancies, through his students and subordinates, and by example. His contributions take on even greater significance when viewed in the context of the time and environment in which they were made. Often Wilson's most valuable concepts were developed in the face of political pressure to move cautiously in a field characterized by corruption and inefficiency.

The list of Wilsonian "firsts" is striking, primarily because they span such a wide spectrum of endeavors. In the area of philosophy, his most noteworthy contribution was the Law Enforcement Code of Ethics. Almost as important as its birth was Wilson's resolve to apply disciplinary penalties for violations. Today's version of his Code of Ethics is a lofty document, which commits police officers to high ideals but does not contain sanctions for transgressions. In any event, Wilson was its original author, as well as its willing enforcer.

Wilson's crusade against corruption has been well documented. His dogged persistence in weeding out bad policemen is legendary. He utilized every means at his disposal to identify corrupt officers, including the polygraph, psychological evaluations, aggressive internal investigative units, and highly restrictive personnel policies. He never wavered in his belief that police corruption was fostered in an environment where politicians were allowed to influence the affairs of a police department. He went to extraordinary lengths to insulate himself from politicians, and in so doing furnished municipal police chiefs with an example which has now become dogma in the field.

Insofar as education was concerned, he was one of many who subscribed to the idea of college-educated policemen, but he was one of only a few who actually conceived a blueprint for an undergraduate program. The systemic approach to education, in which criminal justice students are grouped together in the same academic discipline, was not immediately accepted as legitimate, but now represents the dominant approach. Law enforcement and academia were drawn closer by Wilson's police cadet idea, and by his insistence on bringing the resources of educational institutions to bear on police problems.

An early champion of police training, O. W. Wilson was pressing for state training standards some thirty-five years before the President's Commission on Law Enforcement recommended the idea. To Wilson, every void in a policeman's work routine should be filled by training, whether it was roll-call training, crab meetings, seminars, or impromptu lectures.

Wilson spent much of his professional life attempting to develop a police technology. Record keeping, communications, and data processing were all perfected to a hitherto unknown level. He reinforced technological advances with statistical studies which questioned, and often rejected, practices which had become accepted in law enforcement, such as the use of two-man patrol cars, walking patrolmen, and M. O. files.

Wilson's greatest attribute was probably personal integrity. By his very demeanor, he instilled community confidence in the correctness of his positions and in his honesty. People supported Wilson because he was able to convince them of his good intentions. Furthermore, he offered dramatic contrasts between corrupt and incorruptible law enforcement, as he transformed dismal police departments into "model" agencies, with the public looking on. Wherever he went, Wilson seemed to have a talent for convincing citizens of his sincerity and integrity.

If Wilson instilled community confidence in his administrations, it is clear that he never fully won the rank and file over to his side in either Wichita or Chicago. He grounded his philosophy of change on the assumption that the core of police reform was reorganization. A well-organized police department, with up-to-date resources and equipment, administered with a firm hand, was, to Wilson, a good police department. Inject massive amounts of education and training, along with an on-going public relations program, into the system of the organization, and the result would be a professional police force. Underlying all this was Wilson's premise that line police officers must be closely supervised, the subjects of massive policy pronouncements limiting their discretion, and consistently threatened with punishment lest they misbehave. Wilson held that policemen, if not closely controlled, would avoid work, engage in extralegal behavior, and would subvert the administration's goals. It is an idea which has been disputed by a great mass of social science research data, which indicates that men want to work and derive great satisfaction from it, and that creative managers will attempt to reconcile agency objectives with those of individuals. Still, O. W. Wilson never questioned the idea that officers must be coerced, controlled, directed, and threatened before they would exert an effort to achieve the department's objectives. He instituted no job enrichment programs, no participatory management techniques.

Wilson's theory failed to allow for the complexities of the human condition. He ruled by fiat, instead of persuading his officers of the rightness of reform. He refused to personally involve them in the department's decision-making apparatus. As a result, policemen felt little empathy toward a man who had studiously assumed an adverse party posture toward them and who represented a cold, impersonal administration which appeared unconcerned with them as individuals. Wilson contributed to rank-and-file alienation by applying ruthless disciplinary action. He may also have contributed to a task-centered approach to law enforcement in which police officers, blindly following orders, functioned as an army of occupation in the community, rather than as a social service agency. The research findings on attitudinal changes in Chicago police sergeants indicates they believed that Wilson's professionalization approach had damaged their relationship with citizens. It may well be that policemen will not act democratically in the community until they are treated democratically in police headquarters. Wilson was not a democratic leader.

His public life was spent in pursuing a course of action which he hoped would lead to a police profession. All his reform efforts were directed toward that object. The cynicism with which he looked on the rank and file, however, was really a tacit admission that his programs did not produce professional police officers. True professionals, regardless of their craft, are those who function well with little supervision, who are looked on by supervisors as a valuable source of ideas, who are treated with respect, and who are allowed to exercise discretion in dealing with clients. Wilson may well have believed that police administrators were professionals, but his every action in dealing with subordinates indicates that he neither trusted nor admired them. Wilson's military method of organization simply did not create professionals or foster professionalism. Yet, despite this failure, he never searched for an alternative organizational model. In fact, he consistently strengthened the command control apparatus, while increasing pressure on the rank and file to conform to rigid standards of behavior which they had no part in formulating. Thanks to O. W. Wilson, this cherished concept has achieved almost universal acceptance in law enforcement. Thus far, it has created an orderly system which has formalized working relationships, retarded creativity, inhibited upward communications, fostered organizational alienation, and contributed to labor-management conflict. Ironically, it has actually created an obstacle to the movement to professionalize to which Wilson contributed so much.

Because of the relationship Wilson made between partisan politics and police corruption, he has been able to convince the law enforcement establishment that there is virtue in police autonomy. That many politicians have corrupted their police departments is inarguable. However, the notion of eliminating political oversight from police operations is alien to the concept of American democracy. Policemen must be answerable to higher authority, even if it increases the possibility of venal corruption. A community must be protected from, as well as by, its police department. Safeguards, in the form of police accountability to elected public officials, are a reasonable protection against unrestrained police action. Policing is much too critical an undertaking to be left completely to policemen. Thus, police autonomy is not a virtue, but a vice.

Because of Wilson's penchant for orderliness and precision, and the importance he placed in a formal structured environment, he often became preoccupied with mundane organizational matters. He seemed to spend an inordinate amount of time perfecting the paper relationships on an organization chart rather than interpersonal relationships in the department and in the community. He subscribed to a "by the numbers" method of leadership which assumed that complex human problems, such as prejudice, could be controlled by articulating a policy prohibiting its manifestations. Such policy may have been necessary, but as an adjunct to human relations and psychological training, not as a replacement of them. Wilson often became so concerned with impressing citizens and the media with his reform efforts that he placed too much stock in new buildings, computers, and hardware. The result was a continuing program of selling an image of reform without engaging in the in-depth reform needed to cure the malaise which gripped the police departments administered by Wilson. He never ignored problems; nevertheless, he was often too occupied with superficial reorganization to notice them.

Another Wilsonian inclination was to simplify the nature of crime and the causes of community conflict which, to him, could be solved by aggressive police action and firm courts. Within this context, then, Wilson never truly understood the dynamics of community behavior. He tended to see the police department as an apparatus and the community as the field in which it operated. This is not to say that O. W. Wilson was totally oblivious to community problems. His relationship with Martin Luther King belied that. Yet, even in this case, it is readily apparent that he was intent on "handling" King in a manner which would reflect credit on the Chicago Police Department.

O. W. Wilson may well have placed too high a premium on loyalty. He sensed that one should not argue with or challenge higher authority. Admittedly, this quality had been instilled in him during childhood, and reinforced throughout his career. To Wilson, loyalty equated to obedience, and persons in power had a right to demand it. He felt that he simply did not have the right to question orders, whether they were given by Mayor Israel, General Clay, President Kerr, or Mayor Daley. Wilson's acquiescence was a weakness. Good commanders do occasionally argue with their superiors, and expect loyal subordinates to argue with them. Nevertheless, O. W. never subscribed to this notion.

O. W. Wilson's conception of police excellence was quite narrow. It involved more changes in form than in substance. He initiated planning, installed records, completely reorganized the departmental structure, lengthened training, emphasized college education, and instituted communications. Given all of this, Wilson thought, the department would then come alive. He was right, to a degree. In a badly demoralized, corrupt police agency, law enforcement could be given a quantum boost along the road to professionalization in this way. Yet, a beautiful-looking police department is not necessarily a professional one. Wilson was an expert at constructing the superstructure on which substantive reform could be built. Unfortunately, O. W. mistook the foundation that he laid as true reform. It may have been his most serious shortcoming.

O. W. Wilson was innovative, creative, honest, and dedicated. He always put forth a maximum effort. Many of his ideas have stood the test of time. He developed concepts of lasting value. He represented a moral force around which communities rallied during troubled times.

He showed that police reform was possible and desirable. He was a pioneer who traversed previously uncharted ground, a man who was not afraid to experiment. Wilson had serious limitations, yet his record of accomplishments has been unsurpassed. Contemporary law enforcement administrators and scholars owe him a great deal. But they can best serve their field not by blindly emulating Wilson, but by building on and adapting to contemporary times the considerable body of knowledge he contributed.

Orlando Winfield Wilson was the greatest police authority America has yet produced. This distinction is as much a compliment to Wilson as it is a commentary on a field which could produce no one better.

APPENDIXES

1. SQUARE DEAL CODE

TO SERVE ON THE SQUARE: to be a friend to MAN; to protect citizens and guests, safeguard lives, guarantee liberty, and assist in the peaceful pursuit of happiness; to be honest, kind, strong, and true, always proud of our department and city; to give friendly aid in distress; to be gentlemen, practicing courtesy and weaving a daily thread in the habit of politeness, always thoughtful of the comfort and welfare of others; to keep our private lives unsullied, an example for all; to be honorable that our character may be strengthened; to bear malice or ill will toward none; to guard our tongues lest they speak evil; to act with caution lest our motives be questioned; to be courageous and calm in the face of danger, scorn, or ridicule; to ignore unjust criticism and profit by good; to be alert in mind, sound in body, courteous in demeanor, and soldierly in bearing, a comfort to the distressed, a protector of the weak, and a pride to our city; to practice self-restraint, using no unnecessary force or violence; to intimidate no one nor permit it to be done; to take appropriate action whenever an offense is committed; to have moral courage to enforce the law; to be unofficious, firm, but mindful of rights of others; never to permit personal feelings, animosities, nor friendships to influence decisions; never to act in the heat of passion; to assist the public in their compliance with regulations; to save unfortunate offenders from unnecessary humiliation, inconvenience, and distress. With no compromise for crime, to be relentless toward the criminal, our judgment charitable toward the minor offender; never to arrest if a summons will suffice; never to summons if a warning would be better; never to scold or reprimand but inform and request. All this to make WICHITA a better place to live. For we stand for RIGHT, JUSTICE, and a SQUARE DEAL.

WICHITA POLICE
THE "SQUARE DEAL" DEPARTMENT

2. LAW ENFORCEMENT CODE OF ETHICS

As a Law Enforcement Officer, my fundamental duty is to serve mankind; to safeguard lives and property; to protect the innocent against deception, the weak against oppression or intimidation, and the peaceful against violence or disorder; and to respect the Constitutional rights of all men to liberty, equality, and justice.

I will keep my private life unsullied as an example to all; maintain courageous calm in the face of danger, scorn, or ridicule; develop self-restraint; and be constantly mindful of the welfare of others. Honest in thought and deed in both my personal and official life, I will be exemplary in obeying the laws of the land and the regulations of my department. Whatever I see or hear of a confidential nature or that is confided to me in my official capacity will be kept ever secret unless revelation is necessary in the performance of my duty.

I will never act officiously or permit personal feelings, prejudices, animosities, or friendships to influence my decisions. With no compromise for crime and with relentless prosecution of criminals, I will enforce the law courteously and appropriately without fear or favor, malice or ill-will, never employing unnecessary force or violence and never accepting gratuities.

I recognize the badge of my office as a symbol of public faith, and I accept it as a public trust to be held so long as I am true to the ethics of the police service. I will constantly strive to achieve these objectives and ideals, dedicating myself before God to my chosen profession . . . law enforcement.

NOTES

CHAPTER ONE: INTRODUCTION

1. Mike Royko, *Boss* (New York, 1971), pp. 118–19.
2. William J. Conway, "Chicago Police Force No Longer a Joke," *Wichita Eagle Beacon,* 26 February 1961.
3. Peter Wyden, "He Makes Cops Come Clean," *Saturday Evening Post* 617 (21 August 1961): 70.
4. Citizens Police Committee, *Chicago Police Problems* (Chicago, 1928), mimeographed.
5. Interview with Mike Royko, 9 August 1974.
6. *Chicago Sun-Times,* 16 May 1967.
7. "The Rock Takes Over," *Time* 623 (25 September 1974): 20–21.
8. Wyden, "He Makes Cops Come Clean," 70.
9. Interview with Mike Royko.
10. Interview with Ruth Elinor Wilson, O. W. Wilson's wife, 4 January 1974. This is probably due to the fact that Wilson often signed his correspondence this way, and his textbooks listed him as O. W. Wilson.
11. Interview with Vincent Donohue, former graduate student in Criminology, University of California at Berkeley, 25 May 1974.
12. O. W. Wilson, *Police Administration,* 2nd ed. (New York, 1963), p. 184.
13. Interview with Minor Keith Wilson, a high-ranking aide in the Chicago Police Department, 7 August 1974.
14. Interview with Franklin Kreml, a police administrator and close friend for approximately forty years, 5 November 1974.
15. Interview with Ralph W. Wilson, brother of O. W. Wilson, 11 January 1974.
16. *San Diego Evening Tribune,* 5 March 1960.
17. Interview with Lucrezia Denton McMullen, an early friend and fellow student at the University of California, 14 January 1974.
18. National Advisory Commission of Law Observance and Enforcement, *Report on the Police* (Washington, D. C., 1931), p. 3.
19. Interview with Milton Chernin, Dean of the School of Social Welfare, University of California at Berkeley, 7 January 1974.
20. Interview with Ruth Elinor Wilson.
21. Roy C. McLaren, "In Memoriam: Orlando W. Wilson," *The Police Chief* 107 (January 1973): 12.

CHAPTER 2: YOUNG WINFIELD

1. Interview with Ralph W. Wilson.
2. Interview with Mrs. Clifford Dodge.
3. Ibid.
4. Interview with Ralph W. Wilson.
5. Ibid.
6. Interview with Mrs. Clifford Dodge.
7. Orlando W. Wilson to Olava Wilson, 27 January 1921, Orlando W. Wilson Papers.
8. Interviews with Ralph W. Wilson and Mrs. Clifford Dodge.
9. Wyden, "He Makes Cops Come Clean," 70.
10. Interview with Ralph W. Wilson.
11. Interview with Ruth Elinor Wilson.
12. Joe Stone, "O. W. Wilson: A Fresh Breeze for Chicago," *San Diego Evening Tribune,* 5 March 1960, p. 5; interview with Ralph W. Wilson.
13. Wyden, "He Makes Cops Come Clean," 69.

CHAPTER 3: COLLEGE COP

1. Orlando W. Wilson to Lyla Wilson, 5 December 1919, O. W. Wilson Papers.
2. Orlando W. Wilson to Ole Wilson, 31 January 1920, O. W. Wilson Papers.
3. Orlando W. Wilson to Viola Wilson, 14 February 1921, private collection of Patricia Wilson.
4. Orlando Wilson to Ole Wilson, 31 January 1920.
5. Orlando W. Wilson to Olava Wilson, 21 January 1921, private collection of Patricia Wilson.
6. Interview with Major General (Ret.) William Dean, a school friend of Wilson and former Berkeley police officer, 9 January 1974.
7. Orlando W. Wilson to Lyla Wilson, 2 June 1921, private collection of Patricia Wilson.
8. Orlando W. Wilson to Lyla Wilson, 7 September 1921, private collection of Patricia Wilson.
9. Orlando W. Wilson to Lyla Wilson, 8 March, 2 June 1921, private collection of Patricia Wilson.
10. Ibid.
11. Ibid.
12. Orlando Wilson to Lyla Wilson, 2 June 1921.
13. Orlando W. Wilson to Ole Wilson, 31 January 1920.
14. Orlando W. Wilson to Olava Wilson, 27 January 1921.
15. Orlando W. Wilson to Ole Wilson, 31 January 1920.
16. Interview with Ralph W. Wilson.
17. Interview with William Dean.
18. Interview by Jane Robinson Howard with Orlando W. Wilson for the August Vollmer Historical Project, 2 July 1971, at San Diego, California.
19. Interview with William Dean.
20. James F. Richardson, *Urban Police in the United States* (Port Washington, New York, 1974), pp. 86-104.
21. Alfred E. Parker, *The Berkeley Police Story* (Springfield, Illinois, 1963), p. 61.
22. Interview by Jane Robinson Howard with Orlando W. Wilson.
23. Ibid.
24. Interview with Lucrezia Denton McMullen.
25. Parker, *Berkeley Police Story,* p. 31.
26. Interview with Edward Maeshner, patrolman in Berkeley from 1921 to 1924, Chief August Vollmer's clerk, and Wilson's roommate in 1921; 9 January 1974.

27. Orlando W. Wilson to Lyla Wilson, 2 June 1921.
28. Interview with William Dean.
29. Interview with Lucrezia Denton McMullen.
30. Dean eventually left the Berkeley Police Department and entered the army as a second lieutenant. In Korea, he was the highest ranking American prisoner of war, and won a Congressional Medal of Honor for his actions. Dean retired as a major general. He and Wilson maintained contact throughout the years.
31. Interview with Lucrezia Denton McMullen.
32. Interview with William Dean.
33. Orlando W. Wilson to Viola Wilson, 14 February 1921.
34. Interview with Lucrezia Denton McMullen.
35. Interview by Jane Robinson Howard with Orlando W. Wilson.
36. Interview with William Dean.

CHAPTER 4: FULLERTON AND FAILURE

1. Interview with Lucrezia Denton McMullen.
2. "History of the Fullerton Police Department" (1969), mimeographed.
3. City of Fullerton, Minutes of Board of Trustees Meeting, 20 May 1924; 13 February 1925 (typewritten).
4. Fullerton, Minutes of Board of Trustees Meeting, 14 July 1925 (typewritten).
5. Ibid.
6. *Fullerton Daily Tribune*, 25 April 1925.
7. August Vollmer to Orlando W. Wilson, 3 June 1925.
8. *Fullerton Daily Tribune*, 17 June 1925.
9. Interview with Lucrezia Denton McMullen.
10. Interview with Lucrezia Denton McMullen.
11. Orlando W. Wilson to August Vollmer, 13 March 1938, August Vollmer Papers; Fullerton, Minutes of Board of Trustees Meeting, 24 November 1925 (typewritten); *Fullerton Daily Tribune*, 25 November 1925.
12. Interview with Lucrezia Denton McMullen.
13. Ibid.
14. Orlando W. Wilson to August Vollmer, 13 March 1938.
15. Ibid.

CHAPTER 5: THE WEST POINT OF LAW ENFORCEMENT: Wilson in Wichita

1. William F. Zornow, *Kansas* (Norman, Oklahoma, 1951), pp. 155–56.
2. *Wichita Beacon*, 9 August, 25 November 1927; *Wichita Eagle*, 9 April, 14 September 1927.
3. Oswald Garrison Villard, "Official Lawlessness," *Harper's* (31 October 1927): 52–59.
4. *Wichita Beacon*, 29 January 1928; 11 November 1926.
5. *Wichita Eagle*, 23 September 1926; *Wichita Beacon*, 6 December 1927.
6. *Wichita Eagle*, 19 July 1927; *Wichita Beacon*, 28 March 1928.
7. *Wichita Eagle*, 25 March 1928.
8. Interview with Joe Stone, a Wichita policeman from 1936 to 1940, a former *Wichita Eagle* police reporter, and a columnist for the *San Diego Evening Tribune*, 5 January 1974.
9. *Wichita Beacon*, 27 March 1928; *Wichita Eagle*, 25 March 1928.
10. Interview by Jane Robinson Howard with Orlando W. Wilson.
11. Interview with Forrest B. Dewey, a Wichita police officer from 1934 to 1960, 10 June 1974.

12. August Vollmer to Orlando W. Wilson, 19 September 1928, Orlando W. Wilson Papers.
13. Wichita Police Department, *Annual Report: 1929.*
14. *Wichita Beacon,* 14 April 1928.
15. Orlando W. Wilson to Bert Wells, 31 January 1930, Wichita City Library.
16. Orlando W. Wilson to August Vollmer, 21 April 1928, Orlando W. Wilson Papers.
17. *Wichita Eagle,* 13 May, 12 June 1928.
18. August Vollmer to Orlando W. Wilson, 11 September 1928, August Vollmer Papers.
19. *Wichita Eagle,* 13 May 1928.
20. Interview with Forrest B. Dewey.
21. Orlando W. Wilson to Bert Wells, 31 January 1930.
22. *Wichita Eagle,* 2 May 1928.
23. Orlando W. Wilson, "Picking and Training Police and Traffic Officers," *The American City* 18 (May, 1930): 115-18; A. C. Germann, Frank D. Day, and Robert R. J. Gallati, *Introduction to Law Enforcement and Criminal Justice* (Springfield, Illinois, 1970), p. 259; Parker, *Berkeley Police Story,* pp. 187-89.
24. *Wichita Eagle,* 8 April 1928.
25. *Wichita Beacon,* 12 June 1928.
26. Interview with Joe Stone.
27. Orlando W. Wilson to August Vollmer, March 1928, 19 May 1929, August Vollmer Papers.
28. Wilson, "Picking and Training Police and Traffic Officers," p. 115.
29. Wichita Police Department, *Annual Report: 1934.*
30. Interview with William K. Ingram, 10 January 1974.
31. Interview with Joe Stone.
32. Allen Z. Gammage, *Police Training in the United States* (Springfield, Illinois, 1963), p. 22.
33. "War in Wichita," *Time* (6 November 1933): 28.
34. Interview with Pliny Castanien, police reporter for the *Wichita Eagle* during the Wilson years in Wichita, 11 January 1974.
35. Interviews with Joe Stone and Pliny Castanien.
36. *Wichita Eagle,* 1 May 1932; interview with Joe Stone.
37. Interview with Pliny Castanien.
38. Interview with Joe Stone.
39. Ibid.
40. Ibid.
41. Interview with Joe Stone; Wichita Police Department, *Annual Report: 1932; Wichita Eagle,* 21 August 1931, 9 June 1935.
42. Wichita Police Department, *Annual Report: 1931; 1934.*
43. Interview with Franklin Kreml, 20 August 1974; Annual Reports of the Wichita Police Department, 1930-39.
44. Interviews with William K. Ingram, Forrest B. Dewey, and Joe Stone.
45. *Wichita Beacon,* 26 May 1934.
46. Ibid.
47. Interview with Joe Stone.
48. Wichita Police Department, *Annual Reports, 1930-39;* Orlando W. Wilson to August Vollmer, 23 April 1939, August Vollmer Papers.
49. *Wichita Eagle,* 22 September 1935.
50. Interview with Joe Stone.
51. R. A. Van Welden to William J. Bopp, 19 January 1974. Van Welden was one of the Wichita Police Department's first juvenile officers.
52. Interview with Joe Stone; R. A. Van Welden to William J. Bopp.
53. Orlando W. Wilson to August Vollmer, 28 February 1938, August Vollmer Papers.

54. "Police Department Uses Mobile Public Address System in Traffic Work," *The American City* 34 (July 1933): 59–60.

55. *Wichita Eagle,* 8 April 1928, 5 February 1936.

56. Karl Detzer, "College Cop," *Reader's Digest* 66 (December 1938): 99–103; Jack Martin, "Crime Smashers of Wichita," *True Detective Mysteries* 41 (June 1938): 72–74, 100–02.

57. *Wichita Eagle,* 8 August 1933, 3 October 1934, 20 March 1936; Martin, "Crime Smashers of Wichita," 72.

58. While in Dallas, Wilson observed seven officers who had been dismissed for accepting bribes reinstated by the city's civil service commission. As a result of that experience, O. W. became convinced that civil service was a political device designed to shield the corrupt and incompetent. He was to adamantly oppose civil service protection for policemen throughout his career.

59. Wichita men became chiefs of police in the following communities: Arcadia, Compton, and Burbank, California; Grand Junction, Colorado; Greendale and Green Bay, Wisconsin; Hudson, Kansas; Highland Park and Winnetka, Illinois; South Bend, Indiana; Norman, Oklahoma; Kalamazoo and Flint, Michigan; Houston and San Antonio, Texas; and with the Kansas State Highway Patrol and the New York Port Authority.

60. Bill Gagnon, "Youth Framed into Kansas Pen," *Wichita Eagle Magazine* 71 (4 October 1959): 2.

61. Interviews with William K. Ingram, Joe Stone, and Ruth Elinor Wilson; Jay Robert Nash, *Citizen Hoover* (Englewood Cliffs, New Jersey, 1972), pp. 236–37; William Turner, *Hoover's FBI* (Los Angeles, 1970), pp. 218–45.

62. Orlando W. Wilson to August Vollmer, 5 September 1934, August Vollmer Papers.

63. Orlando W. Wilson, "What Can Be Done About Crime?" *Journal of the Kansas Bar Association* 213 (February, 1934): 177–85; Wilson to Vollmer, 5 September 1934.

64. Nash, *Citizen Hoover,* pp. 236–37; interview with William K. Ingram.

65. Orlando W. Wilson to August Vollmer, 21 February 1936, August Vollmer Papers.

66. Gammage, *Police Training in the United States,* p. 68.

67. Interview with Dr. Hugo Wall, 22 July 1974.

68. Gammage, *Police Training in the United States,* p. 68; interview with Dr. Hugo Wall.

69. Interview with Joe Stone.

70. Interviews with Dr. Hugo Wall and Joe Stone.

71. Orlando W. Wilson to August Vollmer, 22 April 1939, August Vollmer Papers; Detzer, "College Cop," *Reader's Digest,* p. 99.

72. Orlando W. Wilson to August Vollmer, 5 September 1934.

73. Orlando W. Wilson to August Vollmer, 6 June 1937, August Vollmer Papers; William J. Bopp, *Police Personnel Administration* (Boston, 1974), pp. 97–117.

74. Orlando W. Wilson to August Vollmer, 8 February 1939, August Vollmer Papers.

75. Interview with Joe Stone.

76. Jay S. Parker to Vincent Hiebsch, 13 March 1938, Orlando W. Wilson Papers.

77. Interview with Joe Stone.

78. *Wichita Eagle,* 8 May 1939; Orlando W. Wilson to August Vollmer, 22 October 1938, 6 May 1939, August Vollmer Papers.

79. Interview with William K. Ingram.

80. *Wichita Eagle,* 8 May 1939.

81. Orlando W. Wilson to August Vollmer, 3 April 1939, August Vollmer Papers.

82. Orlando W. Wilson to August Vollmer, 10 April 1939, August Vollmer Papers.

83. Orlando W. Wilson to August Vollmer, 18 May 1939, August Vollmer Papers.

84.　Orlando W. Wilson to August Vollmer, 16 May 1939, August Vollmer Papers.
85.　Interview with William K. Ingram.
86.　Orlando W. Wilson to August Vollmer, 18 May 1939, August Vollmer Papers.

CHAPTER 6: THE WAR YEARS

1.　International City Managers' Association, *Municipal Police Adminstration,* 5th ed. (Washington, 1961), p. 10.
2.　Orlando W. Wilson to August Vollmer, 2 June 1939, August Vollmer Papers.
3.　Orlando W. Wilson to August Vollmer, 16 June 1939, August Vollmer Papers; O. W. Wilson, *Distribution of Police Patrol Force* (Chicago, 1941).
4.　Eliot Ness, "Foreword," in Wilson, *Distribution of Police Patrol Force.*
5.　Orlando W. Wilson to August Vollmer, 16 June 1939.
6.　John P. Kenney, *The California Police* (Springfield, Illinois, 1964), p. 91.
7.　A. M. Kidd, "Memorandum on Criminology," 27 March 1939, O. W. Wilson Papers.
8.　Robert G. Sproul to O. W. Wilson, 19 June 1939, O. W. Wilson Papers; David P. Barrows to O. W. Wilson, 6 July 1939, O. W. Wilson Papers; O. W. Wilson to Robert G. Sproul, 24 July 1939, O. W. Wilson Papers; Kenney, *The California Police,* p. 92.
9.　Donald Stone to To Whom It May Concern, 23 December 1942, O. W. Wilson Papers.
10.　O. W. Wilson to Alfred MacDonald, 21 August 1939, O. W. Wilson Papers.
11.　Interview with Lucrezia Denton McMullen.
12.　International City Manager's Association, *Municipal Police Administration,* 7th ed. (Washington, 1970), p. vii.
13.　O. W. Wilson to David P. Barrows, 28 July 1939, O. W. Wilson Papers; interview with Milton Chernin, 5 January 1974.
14.　Joe Harris to O. W. Wilson, 7 November 1942, O. W. Wilson Papers.
15.　O. W. Wilson to General C. W. Wickersham, 1 December 1942, O. W. Wilson Papers.
16.　David P. Barrows to General C. W. Wickersham, 3 December 1942; Donald Stone to To Whom It May Concern, 23 December 1942, O. W. Wilson Papers.
17.　O. W. Wilson to August Vollmer, 26 January, 10 March 1943, August Vollmer Papers.
18.　*Wichita Eagle,* 11 November 1943.
19.　Interview with Minor Keith Wilson.
20.　Ibid.
21.　Interview with Milton Chernin; O. W. Wilson to August Vollmer, 6 May 1945, August Vollmer Papers.
22.　Interview with Minor Keith Wilson.
23.　Wyden, "He Makes Cops Come Clean," 70; O. W. Wilson to August Vollmer, 6 May 1945.
24.　Interview with Minor Keith Wilson.
25.　Ibid.
26.　Ibid.
27.　Ibid.
28.　Ibid.
29.　O. W. Wilson to August Vollmer, 24 May 1946, August Vollmer Papers; O. W. Wilson to Robert G. Sproul, 11 May 1946, O. W. Wilson Papers; O. W. Wilson to Frank Russell, 11 May 1946, O. W. Wilson Papers.
30.　O. W. Wilson to August Vollmer, 16 June 1947, August Vollmer Papers.
31.　O. W. Wilson to August Vollmer, 1 April 1947, August Vollmer Papers.

CHAPTER 7: RETURN TO BERKELEY

1. O. W. Wilson to August Vollmer, 16 January 1947, August Vollmer Papers; interview with John Holstrom, 7 January 1974.
2. School of Criminology, University of California, *Bulletin: 1955-56,* p. 10.
3. Interview with John Holstrom.
4. Interviews with Ruth Elinor Wilson and John Holstrom; School of Criminology, *Bulletin: 1955-56,* p. 10.
5. Interview with Austin H. MacCormick, 11 March 1974.
6. E. Herbert Waentig to O. W. Wilson, 11 July 1949, O. W. Wilson Papers; interview with Ruth Elinor Wilson.
7. Interview with Roy C. McLaren, co-author of *Police Administration* (3rd ed.), 20 August 1974.
8. Interview with Vincent Donohue, a former student, 25 May 1974.
9. Interview with Ruth Elinor Wilson.
10. Ibid.
11. Bopp and Schultz, *A Short History of American Law Enforcement,* p. 118; interview with Ruth Elinor Wilson.
12. Interview with John Holstrom.
13. Interview with Herman Goldstein, 7 August 1974.
14. Ibid.
15. Interview with John Holstrom.
16. Parker, *Berkeley Police,* p. 188; interview with John Holstrom; Kenney, *California Police,* p. 87.
17. Interview by Jane Robinson Howard with Orlando W. Wilson and John Holstrom.
18. Kenney, *California Police,* p. 92.
19. Interview with John Holstrom.
20. Ibid.
21. Interviews with Austin H. MacCormick and Ruth Elinor Wilson.
22. Clark Kerr to O. W. Wilson, 20 June 1957; Wilson to Kerr, 28 October 1957, O. W. Wilson Papers.
23. Clark Kerr to O. W. Wilson, 18 November 1957; O. W. Wilson to Austin MacCormick, 5 February 1958; Clark Kerr to O. W. Wilson, 12 August 1958, O. W. Wilson Papers; *Daily Californian,* 6 October 1959.
24. O. W. Wilson, "Reply by the School of Criminology to the Cline Report" (Berkeley, 20 August 1959), mimeographed.
25. Interviews with Austin H. MacCormick, Ruth Elinor Wilson, and John Holstrom; Wilson, "Reply by the School of Criminology."
26. Richard McGee to Stanley Mosk, 27 November 1959, O. W. Wilson Papers; interviews with Austin H. MacCormick, John Holstrom, and Ruth Elinor Wilson.
27. Interview with Ruth Elinor Wilson.

CHAPTER 8: A PURITAN IN BABYLON

1. Citizen's Police Committee, *Chicago Police Problems* (Chicago, 1928), mimeographed.
2. Wyden, "He Makes Cops Come Clean," 69; Mike Royko, *Boss* (New York, 1971), pp. 107-14.
3. William V. Shannon, *The American Irish* (New York, 1963), pp. 60-67.
4. Royko, *Boss,* pp. 109-12; interview with Franklin Kreml.
5. Ralph Lee Smith, *The Tarnished Badge* (New York, 1965), pp. 157-73.
6. Royko, *Boss,* p. 117.
7. Interview with Franklin Kreml, Vice-Chairman of the Search Committee.
8. *Chicago's American,* 23 January 1960.

9.   Interviews with Franklin Kreml and Mike Royko.
10.   *Chicago Tribune*, 23 January 1960.
11.   O. W. Wilson to Mayor Richard J. Daley, 22 February 1960, O. W. Wilson Papers; interview with Franklin Kreml.
12.   Ibid.
13.   Ibid.
14.   The committee chose two candidates so that they would have one to fall back on if the first choice declined the commissionership.
15.   Interview with Franklin Kreml.
16.   Ibid.
17.   Ibid.
18.   Ibid.
19.   *Chicago Sun-Times*, 23 February 1960.
20.   Ibid.
21.   *Chicago Tribune*, 23 February 1960.
22.   *Chicago Daily News*, 23 February 1960.
23.   Interview with John Holstrom.
24.   For example, during Wilson's seven-year superintendency, no Chicago police officer would be invited to attend the FBI's National Academy.
25.   Interview with Ruth Elinor Wilson.
26.   Interview with Minor Keith Wilson.
27.   Ibid.
28.   Interview with Mike Royko.
29.   Jack Star, "Chicago Shows the Way to Police Reform," *Look* 604 (19 October 1965): 21; Interview with Minor Keith Wilson.
30.   *Akron Beacon-Journal*, 4 September 1962; interview with Minor Keith Wilson.
31.   Interview with Mike Royko.
32.   *Chicago Daily News*, 3 March 1960; interviews with Franklin Kreml and Minor Keith Wilson.
33.   *Chicago's American*, 4 March 1960; *Chicago Daily News*, 5 March 1960; *Chicago Tribune*, 28 March 1960.
34.   Interview with Minor Keith Wilson; *Chicago Sun-Times*, 28 April 1960.
35.   Interviews with Minor Keith Wilson and Ruth Elinor Wilson.
36.   Interview with Minor Keith Wilson.
37.   *Chicago Sun-Times*, 29 January 1961; *Chicago Tribune*, 5 July 1960; interview with Minor Keith Wilson.
38.   William W. Turner, *The Police Establishment* (New York, 1968), p. 114; interviews with Franklin Kreml and Minor Keith Wilson.
39.   *Chicago's American*, 27 June 1960; *Chicago Tribune*, 11 March 1960.
40.   Interviews with Franklin Kreml, Ruth Elinor Wilson, and Minor Keith Wilson.
41.   *Chicago Daily News*, 11 March 1960.
42.   Carey claimed that his association had 9,000 members. Many neutral observers feel the figure is quite high. There was no way to check out the claim.
43.   Interview with Minor Keith Wilson; Wyden, "He Makes Cops Come Clean," 12.
44.   Interviews with Forrest B. Dewey and Mike Royko.
45.   Interview with Ruth Elinor Wilson.
46.   Wyden, "He Makes Cops Come Clean," 13; interview with Minor Keith Wilson.
47.   Interview with Richard O'Leary, former Vice-President and General Manager of WBKB-TV, Chicago, 9 July 1974; interview with Mike Royko.
48.   *Chicago Daily News*, 9 July 1960.
49.   Interview with Minor Keith Wilson.
50.   President's Commission on Law Enforcement and Criminal Justice, *Task Force Report: The Police* (Washington, 1967), p. 172.
51.   Interview with Herman Goldstein.
52.   *Chicago Tribune*, 6 June 1960.

53. Interview with Ruth Elinor Wilson.
54. Chicago Police Department, *The Chicago Police: A Report of Progress—1960-1964.*
55. Interview with Minor Keith Wilson.
56. Wyden, "He Makes Cops Come Clean," 69.
57. Interview with Minor Keith Wilson.
58. *Chicago Daily News,* 13 April 1960.
59. The meeting was held at St. Jude's Hall. It was staged to show opposition to a Wilson plan to shift the power to review disciplinary actions from Civil Service Commission to a board of police captains appointed by Wilson. A special assistant to the mayor, who had been invited to the meeting to discuss the proposal, was beaten and thrown bodily from the hall. Frank Carey was later suspended for sixty days because of his refusal to cooperate in an IID investigation of the incident. The idea of civil service reform created such a stir that Wilson eventually abandoned it.
60. Interview with Minor Keith Wilson.
61. Throughout Wilson's tenure, Alderman Paddy Bawler consistently held that "Chicago ain't ready for reform."
62. Wyden, "He Makes Cops Come Clean," 70.

CHAPTER 9: THE CAPTURE OF CHICAGO

1. Interview with Minor Keith Wilson.
2. *Chicago Tribune,* 22 November 1961.
3. Interview with Minor Keith Wilson.
4. Interview with Mike Royko.
5. *National Observer,* 6 September 1965.
6. Interview with Minor Keith Wilson.
7. Ibid.
8. Wilson felt that since it was critical to his reform effort that he control district operations, it was appropriate that he alone judge the competency of commanders.
9. Interview with Minor Keith Wilson.
10. *Chicago Tribune,* 22 November, 17 December 1961.
11. *Chicago's American,* 25 November 1961.
12. Captains who had previously commanded a district and worked a straight day shift were now being assigned as shift commanders on the afternoon and midnight shifts.
13. *Chicago's American,* 25 November 1961; *Chicago Tribune,* 8 April 1962.
14. *Chicago Tribune,* 9 November, 17 December 1961.
15. Interview with Herman Goldstein.
16. Interview with Minor Keith Wilson; *National Observer,* 6 September 1965.
17. *Chicago Tribune,* 5 February 1963.
18. Interview with Minor Keith Wilson.
19. *Chicago Sun-Times,* 6 June 1963; interview with Minor Keith Wilson.
20. Interview with Ruth Elinor Wilson.
21. *Chicago Tribune,* 25 September 1961; interview with Ruth Elinor Wilson.
22. Ibid.
23. Ibid.
24. Interviews with Herman Goldstein and Minor Keith Wilson.
25. Ruth Wilson tried her best to convince O. W. that James Conlisk did not possess the qualities necessary to succeed in the superintendency. She loathed Conlisk from their first meeting. Ruth was never able to shake Wilson's confidence in Conlisk, however.
26. Interview with Ruth Elinor Wilson.

27. Wilson and McLaren, *Police Administration*, 3rd ed., p. 353.
28. *Chicago Tribune*, 8 May 1963; Wilson and McLaren, *Police Administration*, 3rd ed., p. 714.
29. *Chicago's American*, 29 November 1962.
30. *Chicago's American*, 5 March 1963.
31. Interview with Ruth Elinor Wilson; *Chicago Tribune*, 16 May 1967.
32. Ovid Demaris, *Captive City* (New York, 1969), pp. 264-65.
33. *Chicago's American*, 26 March 1967.
34. At the time, O. W. Wilson was being mentioned as a possible successor to J. Edgar Hoover as FBI director. Hoover loathed both Wilson and Kennedy, so he may have furnished the attorney general with material for his speech that would damage both men.
35. Interview with Minor Keith Wilson.
36. Demaris, *Captive City*, pp. 250-53.
37. Interviews with Mike Royko and Minor Keith Wilson; Turner, *Hoover's FBI*, pp. 172-74; *Chicago's American*, 26 February 1964.
38. *Chicago Tribune*, 25 March 1964; interviews with Mike Royko and Minor Keith Wilson.
39. John E. Rogers, "Crimebusting Citizens," *Parade* (7 May 1967): 16; interview with Minor Keith Wilson.
40. Austin MacCormick to O. W. Wilson, 23 November 1965, O. W. Wilson Papers.
41. *Chicago's American*, 21 December 1964; interviews with Ruth Elinor Wilson and Quinn Tamm, executive director of the International Association of Chiefs of Police, 21 August 1974.
42. *Chicago's American*, 26 March 1967.
43. *Chicago's American*, 9 July 1964.
44. *Chicago's American*, 26 July 1967.
45. Ibid.
46. Interview with Ruth Elinor Wilson; *Chicago's American*, 26 March 1967.
47. Interview with Mike Royko.
48. *Chicago's American*, 30 July 1964.
49. *Chicago's American*, 26 March 1967.
50. *Chicago's American*, 17 July 1966.
51. Interview with Minor Keith Wilson; *Chicago's American*, 17 July 1966.
52. *Chicago Tribune*, 18 July 1966.
53. *Chicago Tribune*, 1 September 1966; *Chicago's American*, 22 July 1966; interview with Minor Keith Wilson.
54. *National Observer*, 6 September 1965; Chicago Police Department, *Annual Report: 1965*.
55. John C. Weistart, *Police Practices* (Dobbs Ferry, New York, 1972), p. 13. There was, however, a disturbing aspect of the study. The sergeants also believed that as the police department became more "professional," the centralization of authority in the department had caused a weakening of the officers' relations with the community. In effect, the sergeants felt that "professionalization" had improved police efficiency but had also served to isolate them from citizens.
56. *Chicago's American*, 19 November 1965.
57. Interview with Ruth Elinor Wilson.
58. Interview with Minor Keith Wilson.
59. Ibid.
60. Interviews with Franklin Kreml and Minor Keith Wilson.
61. Interviews with Ruth Elinor Wilson and Minor Keith Wilson.
62. Ibid.
63. Royko, *Boss*, p. 144; interview with Minor Keith Wilson.
64. Interview with Mike Royko.
65. Royko, *Boss*, p. 144; interview with Ruth Elinor Wilson.
66. Interview with Minor Keith Wilson.

67. Royko, *Boss*, p. 148.
68. Interview with Minor Keith Wilson; Royko, *Boss*, pp. 148-49.
69. Ibid., p. 149.
70. *Chicago's American*, 3 August 1966.
71. Interview with Ruth Elinor Wilson.
72. *Chicago's American*, 27 January 1967; interview with Minor Keith Wilson.
73. Royko, *Boss*, p. 150; interview with Ruth Elinor Wilson.
74. Turner, *Police Establishment*, p. 117; Royko, *Boss*, p. 147; Chicago Police Department, *Annual Report: 1965; Chicago's American*, 27 January 1966.
75. *Chicago's American*, 27 January 1966.
76. Interview with Minor Keith Wilson.
77. *Chicago's American*, 27 and 28 January 1966.
78. Interview with Minor Keith Wilson.
79. *Chicago's American*, 27 January 1966.
80. Royko, *Boss*, p. 150.
81. Interview with Mike Royko.
82. Royko, *Boss*, p. 151.
83. *Chicago's American*, 27 January 1966.
84. President's Commission on Law Enforcement, *Task Force Report: The Police*, p. 181.
85. The marches had been preceded by a riot by Puerto Ricans. The disorder was relatively mild and subsided within 48 hours; but it served to inflame white passions against minority groups.
86. Interview with Minor Keith Wilson.
87. Royko, *Boss*, p. 153-55.
88. Interview with Minor Keith Wilson.
89. Royko, *Boss*, p. 156.
90. *Chicago's American*, 26 April 1966.
91. *Chicago's American*, 14 and 26 July 1966.
92. *Chicago's American*, 18 August 1966.
93. Interview with Mike Royko.
94. Royko, *Boss*, pp. 157-58.
95. *Chicago Tribune*, 24 August 1966; interview with Ruth Elinor Wilson.
96. Royko, *Boss*, pp. 162-63.
97. *Chicago's American*, 26 March 1967; interview with Minor Keith Wilson.
98. Royko, *Boss*, p. 163.
99. Interview with Mike Royko.
100. Interviews with Ruth Elinor Wilson and Minor Keith Wilson.
101. Interviews with Ruth Elinor Wilson and Minor Keith Wilson; *Chicago Today*, 17 March 1971.
102. O. W. Wilson to Richard J. Daley, 15 May 1967, O. W. Wilson Papers.
103. Richard J. Daley to O. W. Wilson, 15 May 1967, O. W. Wilson Papers.
104. Richard J. Daley to O. W. Wilson, 17 May 1967, O. W. Wilson Papers.
105. *Chicago Sun-Times*, 16 May 1967.
106. Gene L. Taylor to O. W. Wilson, 24 May 1967, O. W. Wilson Papers; *Chicago Tribune*, 15 May 1967; *Kansas City Star*, 17 May 1967; John L. Jenkins to O. W. Wilson, 25 August 1967, O. W. Wilson Papers; *Chicago Sun-Times*, 16 May 1967.
107. Interview with Franklin Kreml.

CHAPTER 10: ORLANDO'S HIDEAWAY

1. Interview with Ruth Elinor Wilson; *Chicago Daily News*, 1 July 1967.
2. *Chicago Tribune*, 1 July 1967; *Chicago's American*, 1 July 1967.
3. Ibid.
4. Interview with Ruth Elinor Wilson.

5.   *Chicago Tribune,* 12 and 26 August 1967.
6.   Interview with Ruth Elinor Wilson.
7.   Interviews with Roy C. McLaren and Ruth Elinor Wilson.
8.   Interview with Quinn Tamm, executive director of the International Association of Chiefs of Police, 21 August 1974.
9.   International Association of Chiefs of Police, *The Police Yearbook, 1974* (Washington, D. C., 1974), p. 196; interview with Quinn Tamm.
10.   International Association of Chiefs of Police, *The Police Yearbook, 1974,* p. 196.
11.   Interviews with Quinn Tamm and Ruth Elinor Wilson.
12.   Ibid.
13.   Ibid.
14.   Interview with James Gilbride, formerly a lieutenant assigned to the Inspections Division under Wilson, 8 August 1974.
15.   Karl Detzer to O. W. Wilson, 10 March 1969, O. W. Wilson Papers.
16.   Mel Mawrence to O. W. Wilson, 8 August 1971, O. W. Wilson Papers.
17.   Interview with Ruth Elinor Wilson.
18.   Mike Royko, *Boss,* pp. 209–13.
19.   Interview with Minor Keith Wilson.
20.   *Chicago Today,* 11 December 1969.
21.   Interview with Ruth Elinor Wilson.
22.   Interview with Roy C. McLaren.
23.   Interview with Ruth Elinor Wilson.
24.   Ibid.
25.   Ibid.
26.   Ibid.
27.   Ibid.
28.   Roy C. McLaren, "In Memoriam: Orlando Winfield Wilson," *Police Chief* 107 (January 1973): 12.

BIBLIOGRAPHY

PRIMARY SOURCES

ARTICLES

Ashworth, Ray, "Police Department Uses Mobile Public Address System in Traffic Work." *American City* 34 (July 1933): 59-60.
Detzer, Karl. "College Cop." *Reader's Digest* 66 (December 1938): 99-103.
Martin, Jack. "Crime Smashers of Wichita." *True Detective Mysteries* 41 (June 1938): 72-74, 100-02.
Star, Jack. "Chicago Shows the Way to Police Reform." *Look* 604 (October 1965): 21.
Wilson, O. W. "Picking and Training Police and Traffic Officers." *American City* 18 (May 1930): 115-18.
–––. "What Can Be Done about Crime." *Journal of the Kansas Bar Association* 213 (February 1934): 177-85.
Wyden, Peter. "He Makes Cops Come Clean." *Saturday Evening Post* 617 (August 1961): 67-71.

BOOKS

Parker, Alfred E. *Berkeley Police Story.* Springfield, Illinois: Charles Thomas, 1972.
Royko, Mike. *Boss.* New York: E. P. Dutton, 1971.
Wilson, O. W. *Police Administration,* 3 editions, New York: McGraw-Hill, 1950–1972.

INTERVIEWS

Castanien, Pliny. Interview, 11 January 1974.
Chernin, Milton. Interview, 7 January 1974.
Dean, William. Interview, 9 January 1974.
Dewey, Forrest B. Interview, 10 July 1974.
Donohue, Vincent. Interview, 25 May 1974.
Gilbride, James. Interview, 8 August 1974.
Goldstein, Herman. Interview, 7 August 1974.

Holstrom, John. Interview, 7 January 1974.
Ingram, William K. Interview, 10 January 1974.
Kreml, Franklin. Interview, 5 November 1974.
MacCormick, Austin. Interview, 24 August 1974.
McLaren, Roy C. Interview, 20 August 1974.
McMullen, Lucrezia Denton. Interview, 14 January 1974.
Maeshner, Edward. Interview, 9 January 1974.
Royko, Mike. Interview, 9 August 1974.
Stone, Joe. Interview, 5 January 1974.
Tamm, Quinn. Interview, 21 August 1974.
Wall, Hugo. Interview, 22 July 1974.
Wilson, Minor Keith. Interview, 7 August 1974.
Wilson, Ralph W. Interview, 11 January 1974.
Wilson, Ruth Elinor. Interview, 4 January 1974.
Wilson, Viola. Interview, 11 January 1974.

MANUSCRIPT COLLECTIONS

Berkeley, California. University of California at Berkeley. August Vollmer Papers.
Berkeley, California. University of California at Berkeley. O. W. Wilson Papers.

NEWSPAPERS

Akron Beacon-Journal, 1962.
Chicago Daily News, 1960–67.
Chicago Sun-Times, 1960–67.
Chicago Today, 1960–67.
Chicago Tribune, 1960–67.
Chicago's American, 1960–67.
Fullerton Daily Tribune, 1925.
Kansas City Star, 1967.
National Observer, 1965.
San Diego Evening Tribune, 1960.
Wichita Beacon, 1927–39.
Wichita Eagle, 1927–39, 1943, 1959.

PUBLIC DOCUMENTS

Chicago Police Department. *Annual Reports 1964-67.*
Citizen's Police Committee. *Chicago Police Problems: A Report to the Cook County Grand Jury,* 1928.
Wichita Police Department. *Annual Reports 1929-39.*

SECONDARY SOURCES

ARTICLES

McLaren, Roy C. "In Memoriam: Orlando W. Wilson." *Police Chief* 107 (January 1973): 12.
"The Rock Takes Over." *Time* 623 (September 1974): 70.
Villard, Oswald Garrison. "Official Lawlessness." *Harpers* (October 1927): 52–59.
"War in Wichita." *Time* (November 1933): 28.

BOOKS

Bopp, William J., and Schultz, Donald O. *A Short History of American Law Enforcement.* Springfield, Illinois: Charles C. Thomas, 1972.

Demaris, Ovid. *Captive City.* New York: Lyle Stewart, 1969.

Gammage, Allan Z. *Police Training in the United States.* Springfield, Illinois: Charles C. Thomas, 1963.

Germann, A. C., Day, Frank D., and Gallati, Robert R. J. *Introduction to Law Enforcement and Criminal Justice.* Springfield, Illinois: Charles C. Thomas, 1970.

International City Managers' Association. *Municipal Police Administration,* 5th ed. Washington: International City Managers' Association, 1961.

Kenney, John P. *California Police.* Springfield, Illinois: Charles C. Thomas, 1964.

Nash, Jay Robert. *Citizen Hoover.* Englewood Cliffs, New Jersey: Prentice-Hall, 1972.

Richardson, James F. *Urban Police in the United States.* Port Washington, New York: Kennikat Press, 1974.

Shannon, William V. *The American Irish.* New York: Doubleday, 1965.

Smith, Page. *The Historian and History.* New York: Random House, 1966.

Smith, Ralph Lee. *The Tarnished Badge.* New York: Thomas Y. Crowell, 1965.

Turner, William. *Hoover's F. B. I.* Los Angeles: Sherbourne Press, 1970.

———. *The Police Establishment.* New York: G. P. Putnam, 1968.

Weistert, John C. *Police Practices.* Dobbs Ferry, New York: Oceana Publications, 1972.

Wilson, O. W., ed. *Parker on Police.* Springfield, Illinois: Charles C. Thomas, 1957.

Zornow, William F. *Kansas.* Norman, Oklahoma: University of Oklahoma Press, 1957.

PUBLIC DOCUMENTS

National Advisory Commission on Law Observance and Enforcement. *Report on the Police.* Washington: Government Printing Office, 1931.

President's Commission on Law Enforcement and Administration of Justice. *Task Force Report: The Police.* Washington: Government Printing Office, 1967.

INDEX

Conlisk, James B., 93, 106, 124, 125, 127, 128
Cook County, Ill., 3, 83, 115
Corruption, police, 15, 21, 83, 84, 90, 93, 94, 97, 109, 132, 133, 135, 136
Crab meeting, 28, 45, 133
Crawford, Schuzler, 60, 61
Crime Prevention Bureau, 52, 59
Crime Reporting System, 32, 41
Criminal Justice Program, 74-76, 81
Criminology Advisory Committee, 80, 82
  "The Mob," 80, 82
Cronkite, Walter, 126

Daley, Richard, 3, 7, 84-87, 89, 99, 100, 102, 108, 114-117, 119-123, 127, 136
Dean, William, 24, 26
Depression, the, 44, 48
Discipline, philosophy of, 50, 51
Dugdale, Richard, 34

Eells, Arthur, 31
Eisenhower, Dwight D., 70
Ellis, D. L., 31

Federal Bureau of Investigation, 55, 56, 79, 88, 108-110, 126
Financial problems, 21
Fleming, Pierce, 93
Friends University, 45, 53
Fullerton, Calif., 6, 28, 30-36, 123

Gamewall Light System, 24, 32, 41, 42
Germany,
  de-Nazification, 68-70
  "nominal Nazi," 69, 70
  "Law No. 8," 70
Goldstein, Herman, 77, 78, 89, 93
Goodrich, Paul, 84, 85, 87, 91
Gordon, Walter, 23

Hall, Theo, 68
Hampton, Fred, 128
Hawaii, 79, 80, 82
  University of, 79
Holstrom, John D., 75, 77, 79-81
Hoover, J. Edgar, 8, 55, 56, 88, 108-110, 112, 126, 131, 132
Howard, Jane Robinson, 39
Hudson, Clyde M., 52, 53, 59, 60
humor, sense of, 25

International City Managers' Association, 66

International Association of Chiefs of Police, 8, 42, 79, 85, 89, 101, 126, 129
Israel, Robert E., 4, 60, 61, 136

"Jukes, The," 34
Juvenile Delinquency, 7, 22, 52, 53, 60

Kansas City Star, 124
Kansas League of Municipalities, 49, 55
Kansas State Highway Patrol, 58
Keeler, Leonarde, 50
Kefauver, Estes, 76
Kelley, Douglas, 75, 79
Kennedy, Robert F., 108, 109
Kerner, Otto, 124
Kerr, Clark, 80-82, 136
King, Martin Luther, 117-121, 124, 129, 136
Kirk, Paul, 75
Kreml, Franklin, 50, 84-87, 91

Landon, Alf, 55
Law Enforcement Code of Ethics, 7, 42, 43, 79, 132, 139
  "California Code," 43
  "Square Deal Code," 42, 43, 47, 79, 138
Law of Consideration, 18, 19
L'Heureux, Pearl, 52
Liu, Daniel, 79, 82
Los Angeles, Calif., 35
  Police Department, 36, 78, 79

MacCormick, Austin, 82, 110
Mahin, George, 124
Mann, Theophilus, 91
McDonnel, Richard, 89, 101, 102
McFetridge, William, 84-87, 91, 92, 114
McLaren, Roy C., 78, 129, 131
McSwain, William, 124
Melanipy, John C., 87, 88
Meyer, Albert Cardinal, 99
mining engineering, 14, 16, 17, 20
M. O., modus operandi, 22, 51, 52
Morris, Joseph F., 93, 109
motorcycles, 33, 99
"Municipal Police Administration," 66
Municipal Police Administration Consultant, 77
Municipal University of Wichita, 53, 56
Murphy, Morgan F., 91, 92

Naples, Italy, 67
  Director of Public Safety, 67
Ness, Eliot, 64

DATE DUE